T0290087

The Plains of Abraham

THE NATIONAL BATTLEFIELDS COMMISSION
in collaboration with Hélène Quimper

THE *Plains* of *Abraham*

BATTLEFIELD 1759 AND 1760

Translated by Katherine Hastings

Baraka
Books

All rights reserved. No part of this book may be reproduced or transmitted in any form or by any means, electronic or mechanical, including photocopying, recording, or by any information storage and retrieval system, without permission in writing from the publisher.

© Her Majesty the Queen in Right of Canada 2022

© for the translation Baraka Books 2022

ISBN 978-1-77186-275-2

Translated by Katherine Hastings

Editing, proofreading by Robin Philpot, Anne Marie Marko, Blossom Thom

Graphic design and layout by Atelier Chinotto

Legal Deposit, 2nd quarter 2022
Bibliothèque et Archives nationales du Québec
Library and Archives Canada

Published by Baraka Books of Montreal

Trade Distribution & Returns

Canada — UTP Distribution: UTPdistribution.com

United States

Independent Publishers Group: IPGbook.com

On September 13, 1759, the British Army, under the command of Major General James Wolfe, and the French Army, led by the Marquis de Montcalm, faced off on the Plains of Abraham. By the end of the battle, the British had emerged victorious. Five days later, the city of Québec, capital of New France, surrendered. To this day, the significance of that battle—from the surprise landing of the British troops to the relatively short duration of the altercation and the deaths of generals Wolfe and Montcalm—still resonates loudly and remains imprinted on the collective memory. Often described as a decisive turning point, it tends to overshadow the other episodes in the campaign in North America. And although the conflict actually stretched over a period from 1754 to 1760, it is frequently reduced to that one single battle.

Yet the event itself is only one part of a broader picture, that of a war with worldwide ramifications—the Seven Years' War (also known as the French and Indian War). It was in America, more specifically, in the Ohio River Valley, that the conflict unofficially began in the spring of 1754 as French and British colonial troops clashed over the disputed borders there. Those skirmishes caused tensions to escalate between the two powers, and France and Great Britain eventually declared war in 1756, dragging with them other European kingdoms and their colonies.

For Britain, the objective was simple: conquer New France in order to expand the country's empire westwards. The authorities therefore pulled out all the stops to mobilize the human, financial, and material resources they needed to achieve that goal. It was a different story on the French side. Their country's resources were limited, and were concentrated in large part on the conflicts in Europe, since those battles represented a threat to the very integrity of the kingdom. For the former, it was an expansionist war, its sights set across the Atlantic, while for the latter, it was a defensive, continental war.

Be that as it may, French and British reinforcements alike converged on North America. For the most part, the officers and soldiers on both sides had experience on the battlefield. And in fact, many had previously faced off against one other on European soil. Once they crossed the Atlantic, they were able to rely on their well-trained colonial troops as well as militiamen ready to step up and serve. The theatre of war may have been different, but the importance of alliances remained crucial. Such alliances could influence the execution and outcome of the conflict not only in Europe but across the ocean as well. The Indigenous warriors, with their vast knowledge of the land and their skill at carrying out raids and ambushes, took up arms and supported the regular troops. Both armies were resolved to fight on land and sea to determine the fate of New France.

This book begins by detailing the context and events leading to the first confrontations in North America, which ultimately dragged Europe's kingdoms into war. By that time, tensions were already running so high that the slightest spark would be enough to set the whole thing alight. We will briefly touch on the main events that unfolded on North America's battlefields between 1754 and 1758, as well as on what was happening simultaneously in Europe, since the victories and defeats in that theatre would strongly influence the course of history in the colonies.

However, the main focus of the book covers the period of 1759 and 1760. The Siege of Québec, the Battle of the Plains of Abraham, and the surrender of the city were pivotal events in the 1759 campaign. The following year, the French Army took the winter months to prepare its revenge, which it exacted at the Battle of Sainte-Foy on April 28. Despite that victory, New France's officials still capitulated in Montreal in September 1760.

Although the war began in North America, it concluded in Europe. The negotiations that led to the Treaty of Paris in 1763 were decisive. In addition to bringing about peace, they also signalled the end of New France and the ceding of Canada, among other territories. France's former subjects were forced to pledge allegiance to the British Crown, creating a profound sense of trauma. The events of 1759 and 1760, which symbolized the loss of France's institutions in North America and a severing of ties with the Old World, inflicted a deep emotional scar. The memorial legacy of those events is important, as borne out by the creation of the Battlefields Park in Québec City.

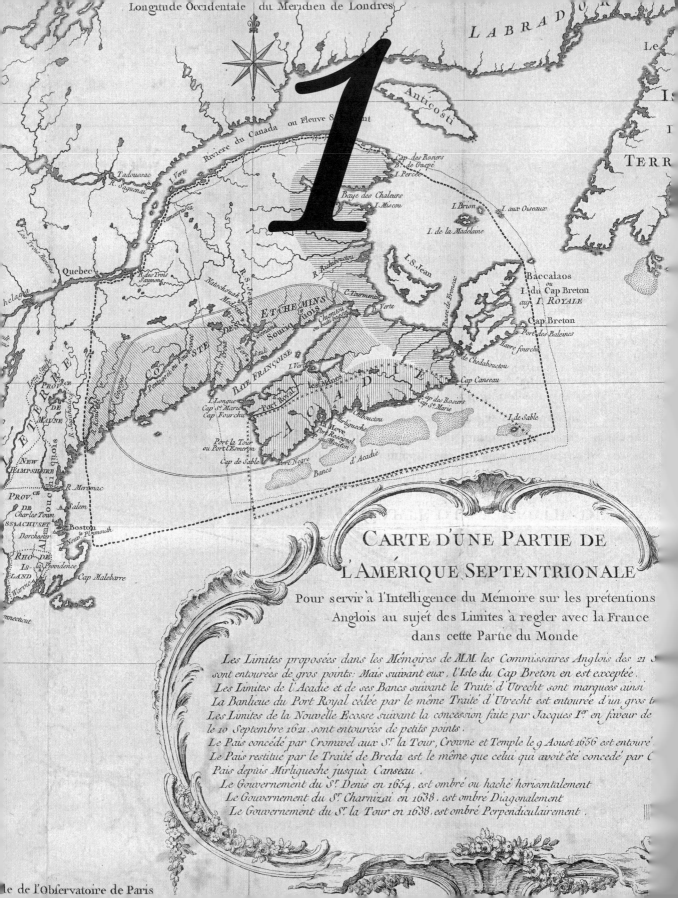

Chapter One

TENSIONS

Enemy Kingdoms

Dating back to the Middle Ages, relations between France and England were hostile, and regularly degenerated into armed conflict, each kingdom viewing the other as an obstacle to its expansionist ambitions. That rivalry was so ingrained that the two kingdoms were often described as "natural" or "hereditary" enemies. In their bid to affirm and enhance their power, the two countries adopted different strategies. While France's sights were set on Europe and on defending its borders and maintaining its army, England, as an island nation, preferred to focus on gaining control of the seas, making the Royal Navy the focal point of its army.

By the 17th century, their covetousness had extended to the colonies, including those in North America, and continued to grow stronger. And by the end of the War of Spanish Succession (1701–1714), the British had acquired Acadia (later to become Nova Scotia), Newfoundland, and Hudson Bay. In 1745, during the War of Austrian Succession (1740–1748), the Fortress of Louisbourg, the gateway to New France on Île Royale, had been seized by the British Army. Three years later, after peace negotiations, the fortress was restored to France. However, the treaty failed to resolve a number of disputes over the boundaries of Europe's possessions in the Americas, and in 1749, a French-British commission was created in order to determine those boundaries and the rights associated with them.

Louis XV had reigned over France since 1715. The country had taken a beating in the War of Austrian Succession, and by the mid-1750s, its coffers were drained and its navy decimated. However, it still boasted the most powerful land army in Europe. During wartime, the French king received advice from his Secretary of State for War, the Secretary of State of the Marine, and the Secretary of State for Foreign Affairs. Meanwhile, George II, who was born and raised in the State of Hanover, in Germany, had occupied the throne of Great Britain since 1727. In cases of conflict, the British monarch held the power in his hands, and was counselled by his prime minister, ministers, and secretaries of State, with the support of the majority in Parliament.

New France

At the same time, France possessed a vast territory in North America that was home to 80,000 inhabitants of European origin, and was divided into three colonies known collectively as New France. The three colonies–Canada, Île Royale, and Louisiana– differed greatly from one another. Considered the heart of New France, Canada stretched from the St. Lawrence River Valley to the "Pays-d'en-Haut," i.e., the Great Lakes region. Dominated by fur trading posts and forts, the "Pays-d'en-Haut" was inhabited almost exclusively by Indigenous peoples

1-1

of various nations, who were accustomed to trading furs with voyageurs. As for the St. Lawrence Valley, it boasted a population of 60,000 people, most of them farmers. These inhabitants were grouped under three governments—Montréal, Trois-Rivières, and Québec—the latter also being the capital of New France.

Located in the Gulf of St. Lawrence, Île Royale—today, known as Cape Breton Island—had a population of 4,000. The colony cultivated very close relations with the people of Île Saint-Jean (now Prince Edward Island) and the French part of Acadia (now New Brunswick). The gateway to New France, these ports of entry were defended by naval ships deployed every year in the spring by Versailles and protected by an impressive bastioned enclosure erected on the Atlantic side of the island, the Fortress of Louisbourg, which controlled access to the Gulf, while serving as a rampart, or shield, to the outposts along the St. Lawrence.

Louisiana, meanwhile, was often considered a colony independent from the rest of New France. Its 8,000 inhabitants were scattered over a huge territory stretching from south of the Great Lakes to the Gulf of Mexico, and it was relatively easy to travel via its waterways. Its economy, based primarily on agriculture and the fur trade, had little impact on New France's economic importance as exports from Louisiana to Metropolitan France were negligible.

In fact, in the lead-up to the Seven Years' War, many French politicians and philosophers viewed New France as nothing more than a financial burden. The sums spent every year to keep it afloat were huge, and largely exceeded the profits it generated. Only Île Royale, which had ready access to rich cod stocks in the Gulf of St. Lawrence, could rival the output of the colonies in the Caribbean. The highly lucrative dried cod market (both local and European) actually generated three times as much in sales as Canada's fur sales, which were comparatively limited.

But New France's real value and *raison d'être* wasn't economic; it was political and strategic. Not only did it ensure part of Britain's forces were kept away from Europe, it also allowed France to slow the enemy empire's expansion in the Americas. Without France's presence across the Atlantic, and the threat

1-2

1-1 Louis XV, the King of France from 1715 to 1774, was so popular in the early days of his reign that he earned the nickname "Louis the Beloved," although certain events during the Seven Years' War would lead to him falling from royal grace.

1-2 George II was the last British monarch born outside Great Britain. During his reign from 1727 to 1760, he wielded greater influence over the kingdom's foreign policy than he did over its domestic affairs, which were controlled by Parliament.

1-3

1-4

1-3 At the height of the conflict over North America's borders, France and Great Britain each had several maps drawn up setting out their respective territorial claims. On this one, dated 1755, geographer Jacques-Nicolas Bellin confined Britain's possessions to a narrow strip of land on the continent's east coast, even going so far as to attribute Newfoundland, Acadia, and Hudson Bay to France.

1-4 An excerpt from *Traité général des pesches*, this illustration depicts the different stages of cod processing, from wharf to drying rack.

1-5

it presented for the British colonies, the army of George II could easily seize the sugar islands in the Caribbean, one of France's key economic pillars.

From an administrative standpoint, Versailles and the Secretary of State of the Marine kept a close watch on New France's three colonies. Management of the colonies fell to a governor general and an intendant, both appointed by the king, who expected his wishes to be respected and who held them accountable. The governor general was responsible for security and military operations, while the intendant was tasked with the colonies' finances, justice, and civil administration. Defence of the territory and its people fell to *Compagnies franches de la Marine*, a troop of regular soldiers. At the outbreak of the war, there were 2,400 of these soldiers spread throughout the territory of Canada and the Great Lakes, with 1,000 others posted at Louisbourg. The soldiers were backed up by the *Canadien* militia, which was made up of every man aged sixteen to sixty. The militiamen were grouped into companies, each under a captain's orders, and at one point, were 15,000 strong.

The Thirteen Colonies

Britain's possessions in North America, while less extensive, were more densely populated. Located partly in the Gulf of St. Lawrence, the island of Newfoundland was home to a population of 7,000, and its economy depended on the cod fishery. George II also controlled Nova Scotia, which boasted a naval base in Halifax designed to counterbalance Louisbourg. Along the Atlantic seaboard, some 1.2 million inhabitants lived in a narrow stretch of the continent, in thirteen mostly prosperous and thriving colonies. In the north, New Hampshire, Massachusetts, Rhode Island, and Connecticut were grouped together under the name New England. The population of these colonies was relatively homogenous, consisting, for the most part, of settlers hailing from the British Isles. Since there was little fertile land in the territory, its inhabitants built an economy primarily on fishing and trade.

In the middle of the Atlantic coast were New York, New Jersey, and Pennsylvania. The inhabitants of these colonies came from various backgrounds, and included Scandinavians, Dutch, and Germans. Agriculture was the main economic driver. Further south, the colonies of Delaware, Virginia, Maryland, North Carolina, South Carolina, and Georgia also practised agriculture, but with more of a commercial interest. Some of these colonies, keen to expand their territory, had their eye on the untapped potential of the Ohio Valley west of their borders.

The colonies were, for the most part, administered by a governor, a council, and an elective assembly.

1-6

The governors were appointed in London by the Secretary of State for the Southern Department and received their orders from the Board of Trade, which was responsible for colonial affairs. Since Great Britain was well aware of the prosperity of its colonies in America, and of their potential impact on trade, it maintained a certain degree of control over them when it came to its trade, monetary, and military policies. The governors were tasked with approving legislation and commanding the militia, which constituted the main defence force of the colonies along the eastern seaboard. Each colony had its own troop, and the militia's structure replicated that of the regular army, which was mostly posted in Newfoundland and Nova Scotia.

Ohio

In the mid-18th century, borders were both a challenge and a priority for the French and British authorities, and the economic success and growth of their colonies hinged on expanding them. Taking advantage of the poorly defined borders in certain areas of the continent (a problem the Commission des Frontières appeared unable to resolve), in 1749, Roland-Michel Barrin de La Galissonière, the acting governor general of New France, began moving his troops into the territories claimed by Great Britain.

1-5 The *Canadien* militiamen were not paid to defend the colony, and had to provide their own weapons, clothing, and even food, on occasion.

1-6 View of Charlestown, the oldest neighbourhood in Boston, capital of Massachusetts.

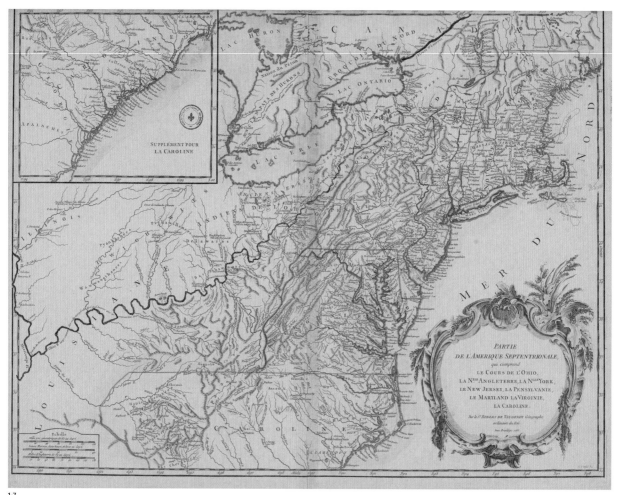

1-7

1-7 This map drafted in 1755 by
Robert de Vaugondy, geographer
to the King of France, shows
the British territories along the
eastern shores of North America.
The course of the Ohio River is
clearly visible.

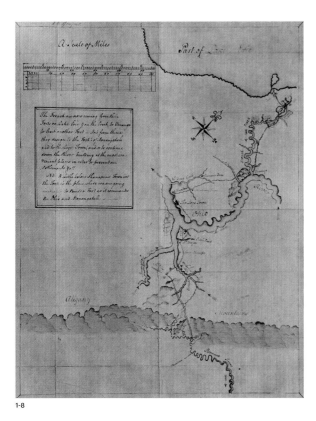

1-8

He ordered his men to the Chignectou Isthmus linking French Acadia to Nova Scotia, to strengthen the French position, and had two forts built there—Beauséjour and Gaspareaux. The goal of this manoeuvre was to confine the British within the borders as France saw them.

La Galissonière also deployed a detachment to the Ohio Valley to bury a number of lead plaques bearing an inscription claiming French sovereignty over the land. At that time, the area was of great interest to both countries, as it boasted land ripe for clearing as well as plenty of game required to keep the fur trade operating. With no documents setting out the borders, both the French and the British sought to claim the land as their own, while attempting to forge alliances with the different Indigenous nations living there. For New France, the Ohio River was considered of vital importance. As an affluent of the Mississippi, the river was the most direct route between Canada and Louisiana. While the French detachment sent by La Galissonière staked their claim in the valley in the name of France, the British colonists did not sit idly by. In 1747, a group of influential Virginians got together and founded the Ohio Company of Virginia, a land speculation venture designed to open up Ohio to colonization. Two years later, George II granted a charter giving the company the rights to land at the forks of the Ohio River. In return, the Virginians promised to build a fort and settle families there, explore the valley, and strike up trade alliances with the Indigenous peoples.

1-8 In October 1753, George Washington was a major in the Virginia militia. He was sent to the Ohio Valley to document the growing French presence there. He noted his observations in a journal, which included this map. Washington also noted the need to build a fort at the confluence of the Ohio and Monongahela rivers.

1-9

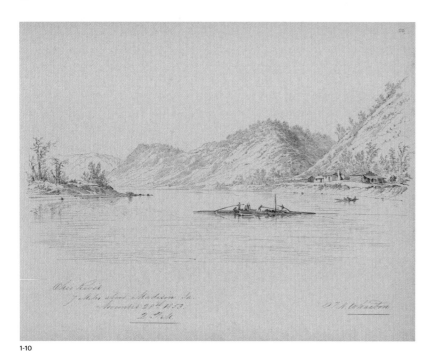

1-10

1-9 This lead plaque was buried at the confluence of the Ohio and Kanawha rivers on August 18, 1749. For the French it was a monument to the "renewal of the possession we have taken of the said river Ohio and of all those which empty into it, and of all the lands on both sides as far as the sources of the said rivers, as enjoyed or ought to have been enjoyed by the previous kings of France…"

1-10 The name Ohio comes from the Seneca word "Oyo" meaning "great river." The French referred to it as *La belle rivière.*

Indigenous Alliances

At the time of the first skirmishes in the Ohio Valley in 1754, most of the Indigenous nations in the region were allied with France and fighting by its side. In fact, since the early 17th century, the Indigenous peoples had forged relationships of various kinds with the French colonial authorities, who provided them a certain degree of support. Meanwhile, the British authorities pressured the Indigenous nations in an attempt to seize their land, and struggled to make allies of them. When war broke out, France was unable to go it alone. It had fewer soldiers and needed the support of the Indigenous nations to boost its regular troops. Furthermore, their knowledge of the climate and terrain, especially in the centre of the continent, was a major asset. But their support was not something the French could take for granted, and it required considerable tact and patience to secure it. It was often only after long discussions and councils between the chiefs of the nations in question and the colony's military authorities that the chiefs consented to have their warriors take part in expeditions and battles.

The French and Indigenous peoples fought side by side against a common enemy, but they fought according to different rules. The Indigenous warriors avoided attacks on fortified positions or in exposed areas that could lead to significant loss of life. Instead, they preferred raids and ambushes, at which they excelled. Their methods of waging war were, however, controversial. The European soldiers were appalled by their habit of taking prisoners and selling, trading, or assimilating them into their communities. And their practice of scalping aroused contempt and terror among the soldiers on both sides, although it was a practice encouraged through the awarding of bonuses and rewards. ■

1-11

1-11 During the Seven Years' War, many Indigenous nations fought alongside the French Army, including the Abenaki, Agnier (Mohawk), and Huron of the St. Lawrence Valley; the Mi'kmaq and Maliseet of Acadia; and the Ottawa, Saulteaux (Anishinaabe), and Menominee in the Great Lakes region. The British, for their part, could rely, at least in principle, on the Iroquois, who also hailed from the same area.

In 1750, on his return home to France, La Galissonière submitted to the Court an extensive report in which he recommended, among other things, that a line of forts be built in the Ohio Valley to halt the British expansion. The French leaders agreed and, in 1753, the forts of Presqu'île, Le Bœuf, and Machault were erected. When he learned from the Virginian authorities of France's actions, the Secretary of State for the Southern Department, the Earl of Holderness, demanded that the British-American colonies do everything they could to prevent the enemy from encroaching. He immediately shipped thirty pieces of artillery to the Virginians and provided special instructions: "... You have now his majesty's orders, for erecting forts within the king's own territory.—If you are interrupted therein, those who presume to prevent you from putting into execution, an order, which his majesty has an undoubted, (nay hitherto an undisputed) right to give, are the aggressors, and commit an hostile act.—And this is one case, in which you are authorized to repell force by force." Despite being ordered to leave Ohio, the French refused to budge, insisting that their king's rights were equally "indisputable."

The Jumonville Affair

By winter of 1754, if there was one thing the British were convinced of, it was that if they were to limit France's hold, they would have to move their troops in first and occupy the land before their rivals could. So, the Virginia militia was sent to the confluence of the Ohio, Allegheny, and Monongahela rivers— where Pittsburgh stands today—to build a fort there that would provide the British a natural strategic position from which to control the area. However, the governor general of New France, the Marquis Duquesne, was just as determined to build a defensive structure at that same site, to complete the line of forts his troops had begun building the previous year. On April 16, at the head of a detachment of nearly 1,000 men, Officer Claude-Pierre Pécaudy de Contrecœur appeared at the fortified structure the British were working on and ordered them to withdraw: "I hereby order you, on behalf of the King, my master, to peacefully withdraw with your

1-12

1-12 After fighting in the Virginia militia in the Seven Years' War, George Washington was appointed by Congress as commander of the Continental Army that faced off against Great Britain in the American War of Independence (1775-1783). He would go on to be elected first president of the United States on March 4, 1789.

1-13 The assassination of Joseph Coulon de Villiers de Jumonville, on May 24, 1754, marked the beginning of the Seven Years' War in the Americas. War wasn't officially declared in Europe until May 1756.

troops from the King's lands and to never return, failing which I shall be obliged, in keeping with my duty, to prevent you from doing so." The fifty or so men occupying the site agreed to leave the same day. Contrecœur immediately began construction on the military stronghold known as Fort Duquesne.

While construction was underway, Lieutenant Colonel George Washington, who headed up the Virginia militia troops, received the order to lead a party of men to force the French to halt their project. Warned of Washington's imminent arrival, Contrecœur deployed a detachment under the command of Officer Joseph Coulon de Villiers de Jumonville with orders to intercept the enemy and force them to retreat. The men headed out on foot on May 23, 1754. Four days later, a messenger informed Washington of de Jumonville's presence a short distance away. On the morning of May 28, the lieutenant colonel and his men encircled the French camp while the soldiers were sleeping.

In his diary, Washington describes the turn of events in a classic episode of war: "I formed a disposition to attack them on all sides, which we accordingly did, and, after an engagement of about fifteen minutes, we killed ten, wounded one, and took twenty-one prisoners. Amongst those killed was M. de Jumonville, the commander." The French version of events, however, differed significantly. In a letter to Governor General Duquesne, Contrecœur describes the facts this way: Although he was surrounded by Washington and his troops, de Jumonville ordered the summons to be read and "Mr. de Jumonville was killed by a Musket-Shot in the Head, whilst they were reading the Summons; and the *English* would afterwards have killed all our Men, had not the Indians who were present, by rushing between them and the *English*, prevented their Design." Contrecœur concluded: "I believe, sir, that you would be astonished at the shameful manner in which the *English* acted; it had never been witnessed before, even among those nations less orderly, to attack and assassinate an ambassador."

In the French camp, the men were out for revenge. On June 28, Louis Coulon de Villiers, de Jumonville's half-brother, led an expedition of 600 soldiers and a hundred or so Indigenous warriors from Fort Duquesne. His aim was to punish and dislodge Washington and his men, who had

1-13

retreated to the south to a rudimentary garrison they called Fort Necessity. On July 3, after a brief battle, Washington surrendered. By signing the articles of capitulation, he effectively admitted his guilt, as the document refers to the *assassination* of de Jumonville. The preamble of the capitulation mentions, regarding the objective of the French attack, "[...] our intention had never been to trouble the peace and good harmony which reigns between the two friendly princes, but only to revenge the assassination which has been done on one of our officers, bearer of a summons." The next day, Washington and his men abandoned the fort and retreated east across the Appalachian Mountains, leaving the site—and the region—in the hands of the French.

Intentions

At the same time, across the Atlantic in Europe, relations between London and Versailles were relatively cordial. Nevertheless, the news from the colonies angered and concerned the two countries, while the efforts of the *Commission des Frontières* continued to flounder. The Duke of Newcastle and Prime Minister of Great Britain was, however, determined his country should regain its position in the Ohio Valley, and he devised an ambitious plan of attack designed to oust the French from their strategic positions, then managed to convince George II to agree to it. To put his plan into action, the duke deployed two regiments of regular soldiers to Virginia and ordered his troops already in North America, as well as the colonial militia, to join them. He appointed Major General Edward Braddock as Commander in Chief of the regular and colonial troops there. Braddock and his men set sail in December 1754. Despite all these movements, Great Britain continued to outwardly claim it sought peace, not war.

When it learned of the Duke of Newcastle's battle plan, France proposed that Great Britain agree to a ceasefire while the *Commission des Frontières* worked out the boundary dispute. But in actual fact, Louis XV was merely stalling for time, so as to allow his arsenals to build enough ships to stack up against the Royal Navy. London refused. The two countries undertook negotiations nonetheless, but the talks quickly got heated. On March 17, 1755, France's Secretary of State of Foreign Affairs, Antoine Louis Rouillé, wrote to Gaston-Pierre de Lévis-Mirepoix, the French Ambassador in Great Britain: "We see with regret, Monsieur, that war alone can end our differences." On March 25, in a speech to Parliament, George II swept aside any lingering ambiguity about his intentions: given the situation, he declared that he was forced to increase his troops on land and on sea, take measures to preserve peace in Europe, and safeguard Britain's rights and possessions in North America. With public opinion firmly on its side, the British Parliament granted a hefty budget to the Royal Navy.

Great Britain, however, had its sights set well beyond its own boundaries in North America. It wasn't seeking merely to protect its rights and possessions; it also wanted to expand them into the very heart of New France. France was well aware of Britain's intentions, and it stood firm. Rouillé's orders to Ambassador Mirepoix were clear: There was to be no compromising on the boundaries: "The King shall never consent to throwing into doubt the sovereignty of the south shore of the St. Lawrence River and lakes Ontario and Erie, nor that these parts that have always been considered the centre of Canada become its boundary."

The *Alcide* and the *Lys*

Meanwhile in Versailles, Louis XV was determined to thwart Newcastle's and Braddock's plans, and authorized the deployment of reinforcements to New France. Six infantry battalions, totalling 3,500 men, were placed under the orders of Jean-Armand Dieskau and set sail for Louisbourg and Canada. On May 3, the convoy of nine supply ships left the port of Brest, escorted by four warships. The successor to Governor General Duquesne, Pierre de Rigaud de Cavagnial, Marquis of Vaudreuil, was also on board. The orders he received from the king bear testament to the complexity of the situation: "[It is important] that you redouble your care and efforts to achieve, insofar as possible, all the objects relating to the defence of your government, that you take precautions to be informed as to what shall come to pass in the English colonies in

1-14

> "We see with regret,
> Monsieur, that
> war alone can end
> our differences."

Antoine Louis Rouillé

1-14 In this illustration dating from 1755, the British lion threatens the French rooster, its paw resting on a few feathers bearing the names Niagara, Ohio, Québec, and others. Meanwhile, the Genius of France exclaims: "Ave Maria, que ferons nous! After our massacres and persecutions, the heretics must possess this promised land which we so piously have called our own."

your vicinity, and that you be on guard against any surprises, but that at the same time, you make every effort in every situation not to let on that you have received any such orders in this regard."

However, the convoy was unaware that it had been outdistanced. On April 26, a squadron commanded by Vice Admiral Edward Boscawen had been dispatched from Great Britain to the Gulf of St. Lawrence with orders to intercept the French fleet and to capture or destroy it. But when the French ships arrived off the coast of Newfoundland, they ran into thick fog, and got separated. Most managed to elude Boscawen and continued on to Louisbourg and Québec, with the exception of the *Alcide*, the *Lys*, and the *Dauphin-Royal*. On June 8, these three ships found themselves face to face with the British fleet. One of the officers aboard the *Alcide* described the encounter:

Between ten and eleven o'clock in the morning, the 60-cannon Dunkirk *came within hailing distance. Mr. Hocquart [commander of the* Alcide*] called out three times in English* "Are we at peace or at war?" *The reply that came from the* Dunkirk *was* "We can't hear." *The same question was repeated in French, and the answer was the same. Mr. Hocquart asked*

"That conversation was the only interlude between peace and the broadside that signalled the declaration of war."

French officer

1-15 Pierre de Rigaud de Cavagnial, Marquis of Vaudreuil, received his commission as Governor General of New France on December 1, 1755. He was the first Canadien appointed to this position.

1-16 Although Vice Admiral Edward Boscawen's mission was considered a failure, the event gave rise to a painting titled *The Capture of the "Alcide" and "Lys," 8 June 1755*. In the foreground the *HMS Defiance* opens fire on the *Lys*, which fails to respond. In the background are the *HMS Dunkirk* and the *Alcide*.

again, and the captain himself responded in a distinct voice "At peace, at peace!" *Mr. Hocquart continued,* "What is the admiral's name?" "Admiral Boscawen," *replied the captain.* "I know him; he is a friend," *to which the Englishman replied,* "And you, sir, what is your name?" "Hocquart." *That conversation was the only interlude between peace and the broadside that signalled the declaration of war.*

The battle lasted barely ten minutes. The British captured the *Alcide* and the *Lys* while the *Dauphin-Royal* managed to escape and flee to Louisbourg. News of the attack reached France on July 18, 1755. Dismay soon gave way to anger. Rouillé wrote to Mirepoix: "Although the Court of London inspired in us a certain defiance of its intentions, we could not have imagined that it would bear such injustice, violence, and bad faith to the extent it would so shamelessly defy the treaties act, after all the assurances the British ministers provided us and the most common of decencies." On July 22, Ambassador Mirepoix returned to Paris without delay, cutting off all diplomatic relations. The philosopher Voltaire, shaken by the events, added: "I was once an Englishman, but I am no more since they have been assassinating our officers in America and are pirates on the seas; and I wish a fitting punishment on those who would trouble the peace of the world."

While a profound anti-British sentiment settled over France, the country seized the opportunity to paint itself as the victim and Great Britain as the aggressor, spreading the message across Europe. In London, Boscawen's actions were considered a fiasco, as virtually all of the French ships had managed to reach their destination unimpeded. For Newcastle, the episode was unfortunate and ill-timed. Failure or not, the attack on the French fleet resulted in a further undermining of peace. ☐

1-16

Chapter Two

WAR

The Invasion

Armed with orders to execute Prime Minister Newcastle's attack plan, Edward Braddock reached land in Virginia on February 20, 1755. He had only a few weeks to put together an operation that was nothing short of a full-scale invasion of New France. Planned for late spring, the offensive would seek to oust the French from their most strategic positions. To do so, the troops would attack the Ohio forts and push on to Lake Erie, where they would join up with a second army and help it capture Fort Niagara on Lake Ontario. Other soldiers would then march to Lake Champlain and seize Fort Saint-Frédéric, while the military men stationed in Nova Scotia would take Fort Beauséjour in Acadia.

By mid-April, the final details of the campaign had been worked out. Braddock had the support of the governors of the five biggest American colonies and their militias. He also had at his disposal an impressive strike force of 11,000 fighters—mostly regular soldiers—as well as about 100 Iroquois warriors. Braddock would lead the army that would storm Fort Duquesne. William Shirley, Governor of Massachusetts, would head up the attack on Fort Niagara. William Johnson, a prosperous landowner from the New York area, would command the expedition to Fort Saint-Frédéric, and Charles Lawrence, Governor of Nova Scotia, was tasked with routing the French from Fort Beauséjour.

But the plan of attack, which had been drafted for the most part in London, was poorly adapted to the realities of war on North American soil. It failed to take into account the challenges posed, among other things, by the varying terrain that sometimes hampered the troops' advance, and by the weather, which limited the duration of military campaigns. Despite everything, Braddock was determined to follow his orders to the letter, and he set out on May 29, 1755. In the following weeks, he and his 2,000 men advanced at a sluggish pace, the heavy artillery they were hauling slowing their march as they crossed the mountain ranges and pushed through dense forests.

At Fort Duquesne, Claude-Pierre Pécaudy de Contrecœur was informed of the imminent arrival of the British. On the morning of July 9, he dispatched a detachment of 900 men under the command of Captain Liénard de Beaujeu to confront Braddock. Near the Monongahela River, some fifteen kilometres from the fort, Beaujeu and his men ran into the British advance guard. Both sides opened fire, and the British quickly gained the upper hand. Beaujeu was killed and immediately replaced by Captain Jean-Daniel Dumas, who decided to maintain part of his troops on the battlefield and disperse the rest to the nearby woods. Now under heavy fire from an invisible enemy and taking casualties, the British advance guard retreated back to the position held by Braddock and the rest of the army. The scene grew chaotic as now the entire British force was under attack from its unseen enemy. Braddock was shot in the chest during the battle, and succumbed to his wound two days later. The British suffered heavy losses, and the Fort Duquesne offensive was a failure. Adding misery to misfortune, at the end of the expedition, the French seized all the documents detailing their enemy's attack plans. William Shirley, who was waiting for Braddock and his men so they could march on Fort Niagara, had to put off his expedition, and was instead appointed Commander in Chief of the regular and colonial troops in North America.

In Halifax, Governor Charles Lawrence had more luck. Tasked with seizing Fort Beauséjour, he assigned his army of 2,000 men to Lieutenant Colonel Robert Monckton. Monckton was the former commander of Fort Lawrence, which stood facing Fort Beauséjour, and he knew the Isthmus of Chignectou area well. Meanwhile in the French fort, with the mobilization of the Acadian militia and the arrival of a number of Indigenous warriors, Captain Louis de Vergor, who typically had only 150 soldiers under his command, saw his troops grow to about 700. Monckton and his men left Fort Lawrence on June 4, and advanced on the French fort. After several days of mortar bombardment, Vergor capitulated on June 16. The following day, the Fort Gaspareaux garrison followed suit.

The British were now in full possession of the region, and the authorities were determined to settle the score with the Acadians who refused to swear an oath of allegiance to the king, even though they had been considered his subjects since the signing of the Treaty of Utrecht, in 1713. And so, on July 28, 1755, Governor Lawrence ordered their deportation. From that day until 1763, over 12,000 Acadians were forcefully expelled, most of

2-1

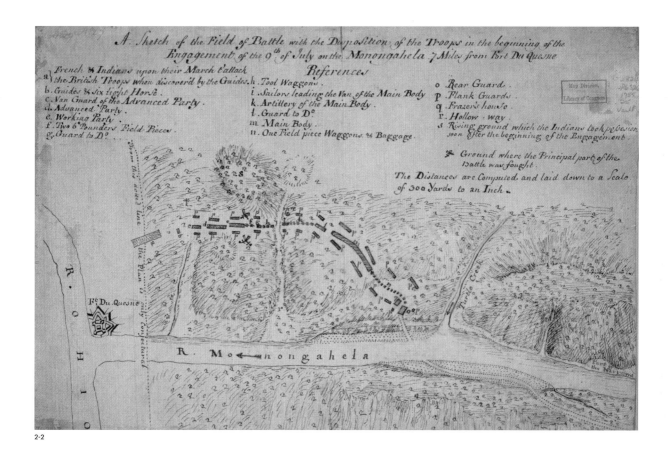

A Sketch of the Field of Battle with the Disposition of the Troops in the beginning of the Engagement of the 9th of July on the Monongahela 7 Miles from Fort Du Quesne

References

a ∫ French & Indians upon their March t'attack the British Troops when discover'd by the Guides.
b. Guides & Six light Horse.
c. Van Guard of the Advanced Party.
d. Advanced Party.
e. Working Party.
f. Two 6 Pounders Field Pieces.
g. Guard to Do.

h. Tool Waggons.
i. Sailors leading the Van of the Main Body.
k. Artillery of the Main Body.
l. Guard to Do.
m. Main Body.
n. One Field piece Waggons & Baggage.

o. Rear Guard.
p. Flank Guards.
q. Frazer's house.
r. Hollow way.
s. Rising ground which the Indians took possession soon after the beginning of the Engagement.

✗ Ground where the Principal part of the Battle was fought.

The Distances are Computed and laid down to a Scale of 300 Yards to an Inch.

2-2

2-1 Major General Edward Braddock and his army on the march towards Fort Duquesne.

2-2 This sketch shows the positions of the French and British troops at the beginning of the Battle of the Monongahela, on July 9, 1755.

them dispersed to the British colonies along the East Coast, while their properties were confiscated and handed over to the monarch's "loyal subjects."

Thanks to the documents seized during Braddock's defeat at the Monongahela River, the French had learned of the British forces' intentions to seize Fort Frontenac and Fort Niagara on Lake Ontario, and Fort Saint-Frédéric on Lake Champlain. Deeming the defence of the Frontenac and Niagara forts more critical, Governor General de Vaudreuil drafted a plan to attack Fort Oswego—known as Fort Chouaguen by the French—which was the British operational base in the Great Lakes area. However, when he learned that William Johnson and his army were entrenched at Lac Saint-Sacrement (now Lake George) awaiting reinforcements so they could attack Fort Saint-Frédéric on Lake Champlain, Vaudreuil switched targets and assigned a light troop of 1,500 men to Jean-Armand Dieskau.

On September 8, 1755, after several days of marching, Dieskau launched a swift frontal assault against Johnson's troops, who were sheltered inside a makeshift defensive structure. After several hours of battle, the British managed to push back the French. Dieskau was wounded in the fight, and taken prisoner. The military operations of 1755 ended with a consolidation of the two countries' positions: the British built Fort William Henry on the site of the last battle, while the French erected Fort Carillon some sixty kilometres away. Both sides prepared for war. As the campaign wrapped up, Pierre-André de Montreuil, the assistant chief of staff of the French regular troops in Canada, wrote: "The colony is threatened with ruin, scores of English to be fought, depleted stocks, and terror throughout the country."

Alliances

In Europe, a diplomatic dance was underway. The kingdoms were aware they were on the verge of war. What they didn't yet know was who they would be fighting alongside and against whom. George II was unwilling to abandon his native Hanover. If France were to conquer Hanover, that would put

2-3

2-3 This illustration showing France and Austria shaking hands is part of an ambitious project carried out by the favourite mistress of Louis XV entitled *Suite d'estampes gravées par Madame la marquise de Pompadour, d'après les pierres gravées de Guay, graveur du roy*. Each image was first carved onto a gemstone, then drawn, etched, and printed.

Ambush warfare
(*la petite guerre*)

During the Battle of the Monongahela, on July 9, 1755, Major General Edward Braddock and his men were served a lesson in what the French called *la petite guerre*. Concealed in the woods, the French Army, backed by militiamen and Indigenous warriors, peppered the British with musket fire, inflicting significant losses. In North America, prior to the Seven Years' War, colonial troops tended to favour this type of battle, considering it well suited to the terrain and to their smaller numbers, consisting, as it did, of taking the enemy by surprise, then subjecting them to intense attack until they fell into disarray. The European officers, French and British alike, believed that, while for the most part, such ambush-style tactics could slow the adversary down, only conventional practices and strategic mass attacks would lead to victory. Captain Louis-Antoine de Bougainville summed up the thinking of the time: "To head off to battle [...] with a detachment, crawl through the forest, take a few scalps, then come scampering back [...] that was what was meant by war, campaign, success, victory [...]. Now, war shall be fought here on European terms. With campaigns, armies, artillery, sieges, and battles." Henceforth, ambush-style tactics, or *la petite guerre*, would become an accessory to conventional warfare. ∎

2-4

it in a position of strength to negotiate, and Great Britain would be forced to make major land concessions to get it back. The British monarch's priority, therefore, was to align himself with an ally on the continent who would help him protect that State. He eventually settled on Prussia, despite the fact it sought to impose its rule on the German-speaking world and had fought alongside France up until then.

Britain and Prussia signed an alliance in January 1756. France continued to negotiate, and on May 1, it signed its own treaty aligning the country with Austria, a power that had previously been an enemy. With that agreement, the traditional alliances were completely reversed. A few days later, on May 18, Great Britain officially declared war on France:

> The unwarrantable Proceedings of the French in the West Indies, and North America, since the Conclusion of the Treaty of Aix la Chapelle, and the Usurpations and Encroachments made by them upon Our Territories, and the Settlements of Our Subjects in those Parts [...] have been so notorious, and so frequent, that they cannot but be looked upon as a sufficient Evidence of a formed Design and Resolution in that Court, to pursue invariable such Measures, as should most effectually promote their ambitious Views, without any Regard to the most solemn Treaties and Engagements.

After having attempted to avoid, then postpone it, France was finally confronted with the prospect of war. It hoped it would be a short one, as the country was well aware it wouldn't be able to resist powerful Great Britain for long.

On June 9, Louis XV declared war, in turn, on George II: "All of Europe knows that the King of England had been in 1754 the aggressor against the King's possessions in North America, and that last June, the English Navy, in contempt of the right of peoples and of faith in Treaties, began to carry out the most violent hostilities against His Majesty's Vessels, and against the navigation and commerce of his subjects." And with that, the war had officially begun. France was in desperate need of money and it immediately began seeking ways to find the required funds to wage war. When it failed in its attempt to impose new taxes, Versailles took out one loan after another, and even introduced a lottery.

Reinforcements

In preparation for the military campaign of 1756, waves of reinforcements arrived from Europe. The British authorities ordered new regiments to be dispatched to the Americas, and encouraged the mobilization of colonial troops. The number of fighters surged to an all-time high, with nearly 13,000 regular soldiers and over 12,000 militiamen joining forces to defend the interests of George II. London appointed John Campbell, Earl of Loudoun, Governor of Virginia and Commander in Chief of its regular and colonial troops in North America, to lead its troops in place of William Shirley. Loudoun was late in leaving Great Britain and didn't arrive in the American colonies until July, which delayed the start of Britain's military operations, despite the efforts of Loudoun's second in command, Major General James Abercrombie.

At Versailles, sending reinforcements was also a priority, but the French had nothing near the same means. In the spring of 1756, New France had at its disposal a regular army consisting of 2,000 men stationed at Louisbourg, 2,000 more based in Louisiana, and a corps of 4,500 soldiers in Canada. Those forces were in addition to the *Canadien* militia and Indigenous warriors. After Dieskau was taken prisoner, command of the French regular troops was assigned to Louis-Joseph, Marquis de Montcalm. His new staff included Brigadier and Second-in-Command François-Gaston de Lévis, Colonel François-Charles de Bourlamaque, and Captain and Aide-de-camp Louis-Antoine de Bougainville.

Like Dieskau before him, Montcalm's powers were limited. The command system in place in New France meant that while the execution of operations fell to the commander of the French troops, the preparation of those orders was the prerogative of the colony's governor general. The king's instructions in this regard were unambiguous: "Sieur Marquis de Montcalm need only execute, and order the troops in his command to execute, every order given him by the governor general." The relations and cooperation

THE ENGLISH LION DISMEMBER'D
Or the Voice of the Public for an enquiry into the loss of Minorca — with Ad.ʳ B__g's plea before his Examiners.

Publish'd according to Act of Parliament.   Sold by the Printsellers of London & Westminster.

2-5

2-5 In response to the British land and sea attacks, France decided to take aim at the Menorca naval base, one of the pillars of Great Britain's defence system in the Mediterranean. On May 20, 1756, two days into the war, and after a naval battle, Menorca capitulated. The British lion was dismembered.

between the two men were therefore paramount. Moreover, the king demanded of Montcalm that he "not only take great care to avoid any such action that might lead to the slightest altercation between himself and Sieur de Vaudreuil, but also to employ his full attention to establishing and maintaining good intelligence, which is necessary between them to guarantee the success of the operations [...]. He shall also be mindful of taking all the necessary measures in order to ensure that the ground troops and the colony's troops unite in harmony."

Because of Loudoun's tardiness in reaching the shores of New France, a sense of restlessness fell over the British camp, and the troops began to be demobilized. Taking advantage of the situation, Vaudreuil revived his plan to attack Fort Oswego on Lake Ontario, a plan he had been forced to abandon the previous year. He promptly dispatched Montcalm at the head of an army of 3,500 men to the fort, which was defended by a garrison of 1,500 men. After an intense bombardment, the British surrendered on August 14, handing Montcalm his first victory on North American soil, along with ships, weapons, munitions, and provisions, and giving his army a crucial strategic advantage, namely control of Lake Ontario. The victory signalled the end of the 1756 campaign.

However, in the French camp, that success was tempered by the sobering news of meagre harvests in Canada. In September, Bougainville wrote: "Since it has been a very poor year, the people have been adding peas to their flour to make bread [...]. An official order has been passed here [in Québec] stipulating that bread shall only be distributed to the population in the afternoons. I have seen with my own eyes this distribution. It is the very image of famine." Provisions were in such short supply that the upcoming campaign would have to be shortened. And so began a supply problem that would only worsen in the following years.

2-6

Failure and Victory

In London, the loss of Oswego was one failure too many for Prime Minister Newcastle, who stepped down and was replaced by the Duke of Devonshire.

2-6 After distinguishing himself during the War of the Austrian Succession, Louis-Joseph de Montcalm was put in command of France's troops in North America in March 1756.

2-7 The battle of Fort William Henry, which took place in August 1757, inspired American author James Fenimore Cooper to write his celebrated novel *The Last of the Mohicans* (1826).

With that, the Secretary of State for the Southern Department, William Pitt, became the strongman of the new cabinet. No one in France or in North America had any doubts about Pitt's intentions. The Duc de Belle-Isle, France's Minister of State, wrote: "He is determined to conduct their primary efforts in North America. He seeks, regardless of the price, to seize the upper hand once again." In Halifax, Governor Charles Lawrence felt that Pitt was set on "carrying on the war with the utmost vigour in North America." Pitt was, indeed, determined to go on the offensive, and he immediately decided to increase the number of men in the regular forces by 6,000 and to attack the heart of New France, tasking Loudoun with planning an expedition against the Fortress of Louisbourg, then marching on Québec.

By June 1757, soldiers and sailors were making their way to Halifax, where an ever-expanding flotilla of ships was moored. Four months later, due to the combination of the large number of French ships in the waters off Île Royale, the persistent poor weather, and the scurvy crippling the British crews, Loudoun was forced to abandon the attempt to take Louisbourg. Following this new failed mission, the commander was recalled to London and replaced by his second-in-command, James Abercrombie. Taking advantage of the change in command and of the lull in the British troops' activity on the Atlantic coast, Montcalm and his men marched to Lac Saint-Sacrement (now Lake George) where, on August 9, they succeeded in capturing and destroying Fort William Henry. During the evacuation of the defeated garrison, the Indigenous warriors allied with the French attacked the column of British soldiers, killing and scalping a number of them. This slaughter prompted the British to step up their actions and take a harder line as the war progressed.

The 1757 campaign in New France wrapped up with the French Army once again coming out on top. However, the supply situation was still dire. For the second year in a row, harvests were poor, due to heavy rains and a shortage of farm labourers. With most of the men off at war instead of working the land, the crops simply rotted in the fields. By mid-November, the French garrison posted in Québec had been reduced to eating horsemeat. The population was growing restless, and riots broke out. What was the point of demanding that Versailles

2-7

Tension and Discord

Montcalm arrived in Québec in May 1756. Despite being commander of France's regular troops in North America, he was nevertheless subordinate to the governor general of New France, Pierre de Rigaud de Cavagnial, Marquis de Vaudreuil, who was in charge of all the colony's defence forces in his capacity as lieutenant general in North America. This command system was complex and risky, as Versailles insisted on collaboration between the two men. However, Vaudreuil and Montcalm disagreed on the best strategy to employ, and tensions soon arose. Publicly, Montcalm complained about Vaudreuil's lack of military experience, and flouted his orders, dismissing them as vague and contradictory. Vaudreuil, in turn, accused Montcalm in much the same manner. France's victories only fanned the flames of their animosity, with each man taking credit. Needless to say, the resulting mood hampered relations between the colonial troops and France's land troops, as Vaudreuil and Montcalm were, not surprisingly, each inclined to defend their own army corps and criticize the other. In 1758, Versailles turned down Montcalm's request to return to France, instead promoting him to the position of lieutenant general, which meant Vaudreuil was now his subordinate. The discord between the men continued to linger, until it was snuffed out with the death of the Marquis de Montcalm, in September 1759. ∎

send reinforcements if there wasn't enough food to go around?

Breakthrough

In 1758, William Pitt wrote to the governors in America, pledging to "repair the losses and disappointments of the last inactive and unhappy campaign." He tasked James Abercrombie with leading an attack plan that called for the invasion of New France by two armies. At the head of the first, Lieutenant Colonel Jeffery Amherst had orders to succeed where Loudoun had failed, by seizing the Fortress of Louisbourg, then continuing up the St. Lawrence River. Accompanying him were over 13,000 men, escorted by a squadron of twenty-four warships under the command of Edward Boscawen, the same admiral who had captured the *Alcide* and the *Lys* three years earlier. On June 2, the impressive fleet arrived off the shores of Île Royale. The French marine, with half as many ships as its enemy and only 3,500 men at its garrison, were no match for the British forces, and the island's governor, Augustin de Drucour, could only hope to hold out long enough to prevent the French from advancing on Québec.

The siege of the fortress began on June 8, 1758, and ended with its surrender on July 26. The conditions the British imposed on the vanquished army were harsh: The men from the garrison were sent to England as prisoners of war, and the civilian population was forced into exile in France. Drucour had, nonetheless, succeeded in achieving his goal. It was too late in the season for the British Army to continue on to Québec and besiege the city, forcing Britain to delay any further attacks until the following year. The troops stayed busy nonetheless, spending the months of August and September shoring up Britain's control of the St. Lawrence Estuary.

On August 29, a squadron commanded by a young officer, Brigadier James Wolfe, who was impatient to continue the offensive, set out from Louisbourg with the goal of laying waste to the fisheries and settlements in the Gulf of St. Lawrence. With three battalions under his command, and escorted by nine warships, Wolfe sailed up and down the Gaspé Peninsula, capturing fishermen and destroying their

2-8

2-9

2-8 In December 1756, William Pitt became Secretary of State for the Southern Department and Leader of the House of Commons.

2-9 Charles Louis Auguste Fouquet de Belle-Isle, the Minister of State since May 1756, was appointed France's Secretary of State for War on March 3, 1758.

"Great courage, willingness, quick wit, and happiness: such are our only resources."

Louis-Antoine de Bougainville

A View of the Bay of Gaspe, in the Government of Quebec, Situate in the Gulf of S.t Laurence.
1 House on the Beach in which Gen.l Wolf Resided in 1759.   2. 1500 Quintals of Fish.

2-10

gear, and later claiming "We have done a great deal of mischief, – spread the terror of His Majesty's arms through the whole gulf [...]." His mission accomplished, Wolfe, who was in ailing health, returned to England to convalesce.

The second invading army was led by James Abercrombie himself, and the troops marched to Lac Saint-Sacrement and on to Lake Champlain, where they forced Montcalm and his army of 3,500 soldiers to beat a retreat back to Fort Carillon. With an army of 15,000 men, the British boasted a considerable strike force. On July 8, 1758, Abercrombie, fearing the French would call up reinforcements, attacked the fort that Montcalm had taken care to protect with an *abattis* field fortification. Against all odds, the French managed to hold off the attack, killing nearly 2,000 British troops, and forcing them to retreat south of Lac Saint-Sacrement.

Shaken by the defeat, Abercrombie decided to take a more measured approach. He dispatched a detachment of 3,000 men to Lake Ontario, where they were successful in capturing Fort Frontenac, at the head of the St. Lawrence River, on August 27. The destruction of the fort's fleet and its depot of foodstuffs cut the supply line between Fort Frontenac and Fort Duquesne, where the British detachment was headed. By late November, the fort's commander resigned himself to destroy the fort before it fell to the enemy. While the capture of Fort Frontenac weakened the French position in the Great Lakes region and exposed the heart of the colony to a potential new route for invasion, the loss of Fort Duquesne translated into a direct threat to France's presence in the Ohio River Valley. Despite these victories, Abercrombie's humiliation at Fort Carillon forced London to recall him and appoint Lieutenant Colonel Jeffery Amherst in his place as commander in chief.

2-11

Turning Point

By the end of the 1758 campaign, the tide had clearly turned in the North American theatre of war. This situation stemmed in no small part from the deep-set convictions of one man in particular: William Pitt. He felt a strong attachment to, and respect for,

2-10 View of the Bay of Gaspé, laid to waste in September 1758 by a detachment of the British Army under the command of James Wolfe.

2-11 After leading the expedition that captured the Fortress of Louisbourg in the summer of 1758, Jeffery Amherst was made Commander in Chief of Britain's regular and colonial troops in North America on November 9 of the same year.

the British colonists in the Americas, whom he felt had been insulted, neglected, and abandoned for too long, and he continued to devote more resources to conquering New France and expanding the British Empire. As a result, the human and financial resources at the disposal of his army and the colonial troops far outstripped those of France.

France's Secretary of State for Foreign Affairs, Cardinal de Bernis, aptly summarized the situation his country now found itself in: "No more trade means no more money, no more travel. No more marine, therefore no more resources to resist England. The navy is short of sailors, and the lack of funds has scuttled any hopes of replacing them. What shall be the consequences of this state of affairs? The complete and permanent loss of our colonies." In a nutshell,

Great Britain had the means to extend its glory in North America while France was struggling to maintain its territorial integrity on the European continent.

As for the Marquis de Vaudreuil and the Marquis de Montcalm, the two men were well aware that the British Army was only growing stronger, thanks to its fleet that encircled New France, supplying reinforcements, weaponry, and foodstuffs. Conversely, the worsening famine gripping the colony seriously hampered France's efforts to defend the colony, as the authorities had only local livestock and crops to feed its troops and the population. As a result, the mood was sombre. In June 1758, Bougainville wrote: "Great courage, willingness, quick wit, and happiness: such are our only resources." There was now reason to fear for the future of New France. □

2-12

2-12 In 1755, artist Louis-Philippe Boitard caricaturized the decline of France in North America, depicting the British arms overshadowing the French fleur de lys, in the top left corner.

Song for Carillon

On August 24, 1758, the Marquis de Montcalm wrote to his mother, the Marquise de Saint-Véran, sharing with her the lyrics of two songs, including the one below, that he composed after the Battle of Carillon to celebrate the French Army's victory:

Je chante des François
La valeur et la gloire,
Qui toujours sur l'Anglois
Remportent la victoire.
Ce sont des héros,
Tous nos généraux,
Et Montcalm et Lévis,
Et Bourlamaque aussi.

Mars, qui les engendra
Pour l'honneur de la France,
D'abord les anima
De sa haute vaillance,
Et les transporta
Dans le Canada,
Où l'on voit les François
Culbuter les Anglois ■

Chapter Three

THE SIEGE

Resisting Until the Return of Peace

In the fall of 1758, the Marquis de Montcalm knew that only the arrival of reinforcements once the ice melted come spring could save New France, which is why he and Vaudreuil dispatched Bougainville to Versailles to present a series of briefs that appear to have been penned by their emissary during the crossing. In a grave and pessimistic tone, he sets out the colony's needs for the 1759 campaign:

Foodstuffs: *We have insufficient foodstuffs, which is to say that by rationing what little we do have, we shall have barely enough to embark on the campaign and survive the first month.*

Munitions of war: *We are so short of gunpowder that if the English were to attack Québec, our cannon-fire would not last six days. Virtually all the cannons are of cast iron and are in poor state; our supply of mortars is low, and even more so, our bombs of the correct calibre [...].*

Means of transportation: *Lastly, we are thoroughly lacking in every means to act, transport, and march with haste [...].*

With a certain poetic flair, he added, "for he who has never left the shores of Europe, it is not possible to imagine the miracle, and the miracle of creation, that is required to wage a European war on Canadian soil; such a picture exceeds even the most energetic brush of Rubens himself." Concretely, Montcalm

3-1

3-1 Before joining the French Army in North America, Louis-Antoine de Bougainville was secretary to the French ambassador in Great Britain, Gaston-Pierre de Lévis-Mirepoix. He also wrote an essay on integral calculus and was a member of the Royal Society of London, an institution dedicated to promoting the sciences.

3-2

Over the course of their campaigns and battles, the Marquis de Vaudreuil and the Marquis de Montcalm developed two opposing strategies, each in keeping with their respective experience. Vaudreuil proposed an offensive approach that sought to resist by exerting constant pressure on the British as well as on their forts and their borders. He favoured the use of extended lines that could be contracted as needed. As far as Montcalm was concerned, this way of waging war would do little to intimidate the enemy. While he, too, preferred an offensive tactic, he was aware of the challenges of defending such a vast territory, the number of soldiers required to protect it, the costs associated with moving and feeding his troops, and the operational limits of the militia. On the eve of the 1759 campaign, he preferred to consolidate his troops and essentially task them with defending the St. Lawrence River Valley. If he stretched them too thin, there was a risk France would lose everything. By this point, the colony was exhausted and ruined by years of conflict, and its economy was simply too weak to support the war effort.

Berryer's instructions to Vaudreuil and Montcalm regarding the 1759 campaign were unambiguous and in keeping with Montcalm's strategy, essentially ordering the men to concentrate their forces and limit their losses: "The primary objective of which you must not lose sight is to preserve a sufficient portion of the colony at the least, and to remain in control of it so as to regain its entirety once peace has been achieved. Such is the important objective towards which all your views and operations shall be directed." From that point on, Montcalm was expected to hold the St. Lawrence River Valley—and Québec in particular—for as long as possible in anticipation of the end of hostilities in Europe. This meant uniting all of the colony's forces.

and Vaudreuil hoped to obtain a dozen warships, one thousand handpicked recruits, a team of engineers to improve their fortifications, as well as great quantities of weapons, ammunition, and food.

Bougainville left Québec for Versailles on November 15, 1758, but upon arrival he was sorely disappointed when the Secretary of State for the Marine, Nicolas-René Berryer, informed him, by way of a now-legendary parable, that France simply did not have the means to support its colony: "On ne cherche point à sauver les écuries quand le feu est à la maison." (There's no point trying to save the stables when the house is on fire.) France was unable to muster either the necessary resources or the ships required to carry them across the ocean. Montcalm's and Vaudreuil's emissary eventually managed to secure a pledge for two engineers, 24 canonniers, and 350 recruits dispatched aboard two frigates armed with some twenty cannons. As for their food supplies, which consisted mainly of flour, lard, drink, and dried goods, they were loaded onto fifteen ships escorted by six frigates from France's merchant marine. No warships were assigned to accompany the convoy. As consolation, the officers deployed to New France were given promotions.

Québec

Meanwhile, the British authorities were drafting their fifth campaign plan since the beginning of the war and fine-tuning their strategy, which consisted of simultaneous attacks on three fronts. On the orders of Jeffery Amherst, Commander in

Chief of the British Army in North America, James Wolfe was tasked with seizing Québec via the St. Lawrence River. Brigadier General John Prideaux would besiege Fort Niagara from Lake Ontario, and Amherst would lead a third army to capture Fort Carillon and Fort Saint-Frédéric before crossing the length of Lake Champlain and pushing up the Richelieu and St. Lawrence rivers towards Montreal. In 1759, the British were resolutely committed to their goal of waging war in the very heart of Canada.

The city of Québec symbolized France's presence in the Americas, and was the seat of its administrative, economic, military, and religious powers. In addition, thanks to its geographic position, geomorphological characteristics, and surrounding drainage basin, the city had acquired an undeniable strategic advantage since its founding in 1608. Québec was a vital communications link between New France and Europe on which imports, exports, supplies, and reinforcements depended. As a result, it was an integral part of the hegemonic ambitions of both the French and British empires. For London, seizing Québec was a crucial step in its plan to conquer all of New France. But it wouldn't be an easy task, because the city was protected by waterways and by cliffs that were considered impregnable.

On the eve of the 1759 campaign, the British authorities pulled out all the stops to ensure the expedition to take Québec was a success. On January 12, William Pitt appointed a young officer named James Wolfe as major general and commander of the campaign's land troops. Wolfe, who had drawn praise several months earlier during the capture of Louisbourg, was tasked with the important mission of sailing up the St. Lawrence River to besiege and take Québec. Although Wolfe officially reported to Amherst, in actual fact he acted independently, as the physical distance separating the men made interaction between the two impossible.

James Wolfe was an officer renowned for his bravery in battle, but his health was ailing. When he was called on, for the first time in his career, to act as commander in chief, he expressed certain reservations about his new role. In a letter to his uncle, he wrote: "I am to act a greater part in this business than I wished or desired." He would, however, be

3-3

3-2 Nicolas-René Berryer was appointed secretary of state of the Marine on November 1, 1758.

3-3 With the state of the colony growing more critical by the day, on February 17, 1759, the Bishop of Québec published a notice (*Mandement à l'occasion de la guerre*) ordering that a procession be held in every village on the first Sunday of each month.

3-4

"I am to act a greater part in this business than I wished or desired."

James Wolfe

3-4 Québec's strategic value was undeniable. Captured by England in 1629, then returned to France in 1632, the city had once again come under attack in 1690, but this time the French Army managed to hold off the enemy. Then, in 1711, a British fleet sailed up the St. Lawrence with the aim of seizing the city, but part of the convoy was shipwrecked, and the remaining ships turned around and headed home.

backed by an experienced military staff consisting of three brigadier generals. Robert Monckton, the expedition's second in command, had served in North America since 1752, and had led the British to victory at Fort Gaspareaux (French Acadia) in 1755. James Murray had many years of service under his belt and he, too, had taken part in the capture of Louisbourg the previous year under Wolfe. The third brigadier general, George Townshend, was an aristocrat and politician with a strong temperament who, unlike his fellow leaders, had battle experience in Europe, but not in North America. He also had the distinction of being the only one of the three to have been chosen by the government and not by Wolfe himself. Also under Wolfe's command were 8,500 regular troops.

Setting Sail

James Wolfe and his troops left the shores of England on February 14, 1759, aboard a large number of ships under the command of Vice Admiral Charles Saunders, an experienced and competent navy officer. The major general was utterly determined to seize, and even destroy, the city: "If by accident in the River, by the Enemy's resistance, by sickness, or slaughter in the Army, or from any other cause, we find, that Quebec is not likely to fall into our hands [...], I propose to set the Town on fire with Shells, to destroy the Harvest, Houses, & Cattle both above and below, to send off as many Canadians as possible to Europe, & to leave famine and desolation behind me."

The squadron vanguard consisting of ten warships under the command of Rear Admiral Philip Durell spent the winter in Halifax where they would intercept any relief sent by France, come spring. However, with ice and unfavourable winds immobilizing his ships, Durell was unable to prevent Bougainville's flotilla from sailing up the St. Lawrence when it arrived from France. In fact, he was still in Halifax when Wolfe and Saunders joined him on April 30, and it wasn't until May 5 that Durell finally set sail.

Upon his arrival in Louisbourg on May 15, Saunders reorganized his fleet and finished loading supplies. He raised anchor on June 4 and headed towards the Gulf of St. Lawrence just as Durell's advance guard reached Île aux Coudres, about 100 kilometres from Québec. The passage of the British flotilla sailing up the river was an awe-inspiring sight for the locals who witnessed the convoy. Making up fully one-quarter of the Royal Navy, it consisted of 49 warships, 13,500 boatmen, and 2,100 naval fusiliers. One hundred and forty vessels, with 4,500 sailors on board, transported the land troops and supplies. The convoy also included 134 landing craft.

James Wolfe took advantage of the voyage to draft his attack plan:

The town of Quebec is poorly fortified, but the ground round about it is rocky. To invest the place, and cut off all communication with the colony, it will be necessary to encamp with our right to the River St. Lawrence, and our left to the river St. Charles. From the river St. Charles to Beauport the communication must be kept open by strong entrenched posts and redoubts. The

3-5

3-6

3-5 While James Wolfe had drawn praise during the capture of Louisbourg in the summer of 1758, William Pitt nonetheless took a risk in appointing him as commander of the expedition against Québec as it would be the first time Wolfe was in charge of drafting and implementing the plans for a military campaign.

3-6 Vice Admiral Charles Saunders is appointed commander of the fleet deployed on January 9, 1759, to capture Québec.

enemy can pass that river at low water; and it will be proper to establish ourselves with small entrenched posts from the point of Levi to La Chaudière. It is the business of our naval force to be masters of the river, both above and below the town.

Mounting a Defence

Meanwhile, having managed to sail up the St. Lawrence just ahead of Durell's squadron, Bougainville arrived in Québec on May 10, 1759. News of the arrival of food supplies was met with joy by the city's residents who, since the winter, had been reduced to a daily ration of a quarter of a pound of bread and half a pound of horsemeat. Bougainville continued on to Montreal, where he informed Vaudreuil and Montcalm of the meagre resources he had been allocated, along with Berryer's instructions and the promotions that had been awarded. Despite having been appointed lieutenant general,

Montcalm in many ways remained subordinate to the Marquis de Vaudreuil, who was still the authority with regard to the colony's safety and to military operations. Montcalm departed Montreal, arriving in Québec on May 22, where, the very next day, he held the first council of war and learned that Durell's advance guard had already sailed past Bic, some 250 kilometres from the city. French relief ships would no longer be able to reach Québec, and fortifying the site became an immediate priority. On hearing the news, Montcalm opted to exercise caution and implement a defensive strategy.

In the wake of the first fall of Louisbourg in 1745, engineer Gaspard Chaussegros de Léry drew up and put in place a defence plan for the city of Québec that called for the erection of a rampart that would definitively seal off the western side of the upper town where the battle was likely to occur. The new fortification was designed to withstand an enemy siege. It was a permanent structure, as the earthworks were supported by masonry walls. On

3-7

3-8

his arrival in New France, Montcalm had expressed doubts about the ability of de Léry's ramparts to stand up to attack. In 1757, he conducted a reconnaissance mission around the perimeter of the city and drew up a new defensive strategy.

His strategy revolved around one central premise: the only place the British could attack was in Beauport, between the St. Charles and Montmorency rivers, a zone that provided no natural defence. Montcalm therefore recommended entrenching the Beauport coast and the escarpment overlooking it, and implementing various means to defend the Laurentian Channel, including erecting a battery at Cap Tourmente. In a brief he wrote in January 1759, engineer Nicolas Sarrebource de Pontleroy agreed, and suggested a line of redoubts be built to protect the area. So convinced were they that the landing would take place in Beauport that

3-8 As noted by the Ursuline nuns, the people of Québec were ecstatic at the arrival of the foodstuffs the emissary Bougainville had managed to secure: "We were ever so surprised when on May 27 we spotted [...] one of the King's vessels; the joy was so great that people climbed up onto the roofs of the houses and atop chimneys to see for themselves and to shout the good news to one and all [...]."

Fortifying Québec

ABATTIS: A line of tree branches laid in a row and strapped together, with the sharpened tops directed outwards, towards the enemy.

BATTERY: A group of several pieces of artillery laid out on platforms and protected by a parapet on which openings—or embrasures—were made to allow soldiers to fire through.

REDOUBT: A fortified work consisting of angular projections and set apart from a permanent or temporary fortification. It served to shelter soldiers posted beyond the main defensive line.

ENTRENCHMENT: A long trench or ditch dug in front of defensive works and designed to slow the advance of enemy troops and expose them to fire from the besieged soldiers. ∎

most of the resources were concentrated there, leaving the city with scant protection.

When Montcalm returned to Québec in May 1759 and took in the situation, he could only conclude that "nothing had been done, and there were no resources to do it." However, with the arrival of the regular troops and the militiamen from points around the colony, the pace of work picked up quickly, despite torrential rains and a shortage of tools and materials. In a very short time, the city's defences were stepped up, and the Beauport coast was fortified. Redoubts were erected in Beauport, and entrenchments and batteries were built between the Montmorency and St. Charles rivers, while other batteries were erected within the city walls. The plan to build a battery at Cap Tourmente was dropped due to a lack of resources.

Nevertheless, by the time the work was complete, the defensive works covered a considerable area. The Marquis de Montcalm opted to join the majority of the troops in Beauport and make his camp there, at the centre of that crucial sector. Vaudreuil, for his part, took up position closer to the city, at the De la Canardière camp, between the St. Charles River and Beauport. Meanwhile, Québec and its garrison were entrusted to Lieutenant Jean-Baptiste-Nicolas-Roch de Ramezay.

Since the colony didn't have a significant naval force, its first line of defence against potential attacks from the water hinged on the complexity and dangers of navigation on the St. Lawrence. In order to protect the river and prevent enemy ships from circulating freely, batteries would need to be erected on both shores. But given the lack of available resources, this option was rejected by the engineers tasked with defending Québec, leaving strategic positions on the south shore, including at Point Lévis, to the British.

At the same time, Montcalm decided to keep only a limited supply of munitions and food provisions at the king's storehouses in the city. The rest was to be stored at a depot at the mouth of the Batiscan River, some 100 kilometres upstream from Québec. The aim of this tactic was to avoid valuable resources falling into the hands of the enemy if the British managed to take the city, while ensuring the subsistence of the troops that would be forced to retreat towards Montreal in that event. If Québec were besieged, the plan was to have the supplies transported by maritime *cabotage* and wagon. However, those convoys would become impossible if the British succeeded in landing upstream from Québec, in which case the lines of communication between the city and its food supplies would be broken, leading to starvation of civilians and soldiers alike.

While the fortification work and strategic planning was underway, military preparations were in full swing. The regular soldiers and Indigenous allies made their way to Québec, and the Québec, Trois-Rivières, and Montreal government militias also joined up with the army troops. A small, handpicked group of militiamen was even incorporated into the ground troop battalions. But with so many troops concentrated in one place, several of the colony's key areas, including the Lake Ontario and Lake Champlain sectors, were left vulnerable to attack. Québec's civilian population was evacuated, with most of its 8,000 residents fleeing to areas outside the city. In the nearby settlements, women, children, and the elderly sought refuge in the woods, taking their livestock with them.

Keeping Watch and Maintaining a Threatening Presence

Vice Admiral Saunders was able to make his way safely to Québec thanks to the detailed hydrographic surveys of the St. Lawrence River that the British seized from the enemy. Accompanied by *Canadien* ship captains who had been taken prisoner earlier in the conflict, the British fleet was able to sail smoothly up the river, despite the waters being renowned for their navigational hazards. Even the Traverse passage, a bottleneck at the tip of Île d'Orléans, caused the fleet no trouble. After successfully negotiating this notorious passage, one experienced officer who had sailed on all the major European rivers, declared the St. Lawrence "to be the finest river, the safest navigation, with the best anchorage in it, of any other within my knowledge; that it is infinitely preferable to the Thames or the Rhone, and that I have not yet met with least difficulty in working up." The speed and ease with which

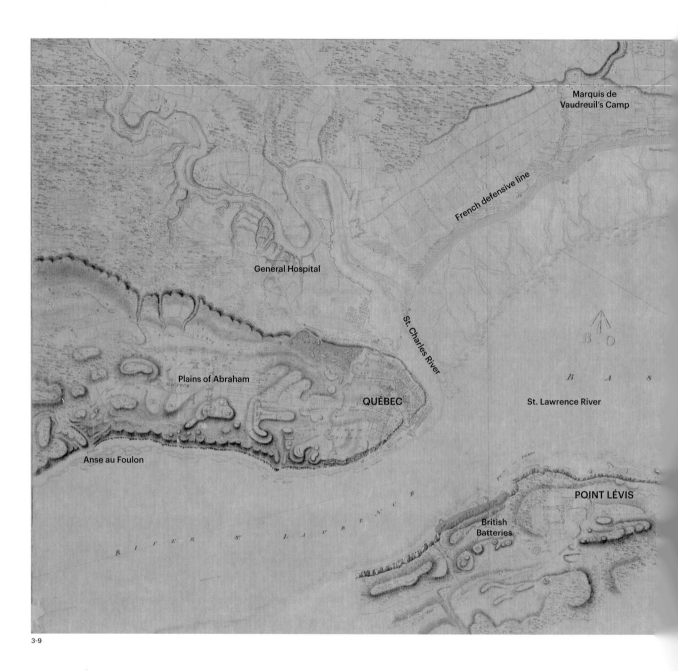

Marquis de
Vaudreuil's Camp

French defensive line

General Hospital

St. Charles River

B. O

B A S

Plains of Abraham

QUÉBEC

St. Lawrence River

Anse au Foulon

RIVER ST LAURENCE

POINT LÉVIS

British
Batteries

3-9

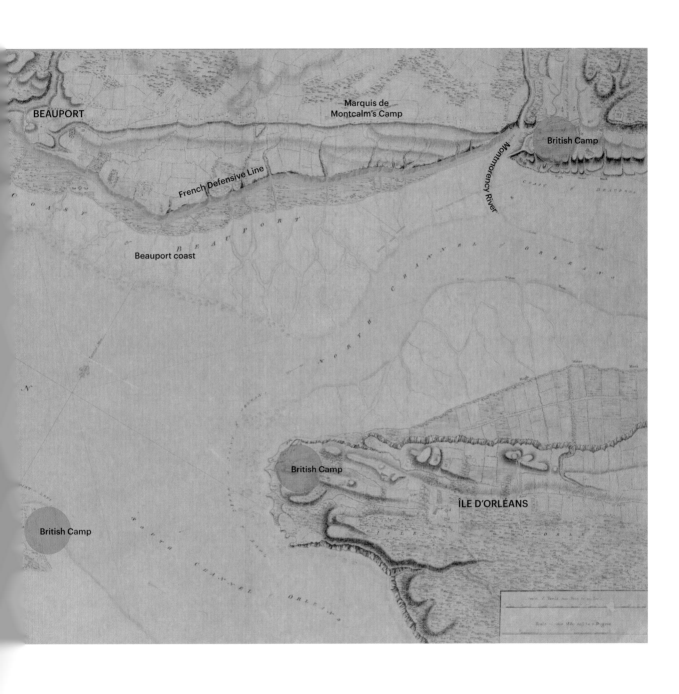

3-9 Position of the French
and British armies in the
summer of 1759.

the British fleet managed to sail up the St. Lawrence astounded the French authorities, leading Montcalm to conclude that "our best seamen or pilots seem to me to be either liars or ignoramuses."

On June 26, the first British transport ships dropped anchor just off Île d'Orléans, prompting the French troops to reinforce their positions in the Beauport area. The following day, Major General James Wolfe led a landing on the southwestern tip of the island, in the parish of Saint-Laurent, which had been abandoned by its residents. Accompanied by a detachment of light infantry, Wolfe reached the tip of the island and was at last able to lay his eyes on Québec. Perched atop its legendary rocky promontory, the city resembled nothing short of a fortress.

But a surprise awaited Wolfe: his adversary had anticipated his intentions. From the St. Charles to the Montmorency rivers, Montcalm had erected redoubts, entrenchments, and batteries, and had struck a series of camps there. The British plan to land at Beauport would be no easy feat; they would have to rethink their plan of attack. Wolfe did, however, note that the heights of the Point Lévis were unprotected and that it would be easy enough for his troops to occupy that strategic site. By erecting batteries on the heights, the British ships would be able to anchor upstream from Île d'Orléans and, more importantly, to bombard the city. Wolfe also decided to set up camp on the left bank of the Montmorency River, directly opposite the French defensive line.

Wolfe's strategy also took aim at the local population, and on June 29 he posted a manifesto (in French) that was part promise, part threat:

The people may remain unmolested on their lands, inhabit their houses, and enjoy their religion in security; for these inestimable blessings I expect the Canadians will take no part in the great contest between the two crowns. But if, by a vain obstinacy and misguided valour, they presume to appear in arms, they must expect the most fatal consequences; their habitations destroyed, their sacred temples exposed to an exasperated soldiery, their harvest utterly ruined and the only passage for relief stopped up by a most formidable fleet.

In response to the arrival of the British Army, Vaudreuil launched what would prove to be the

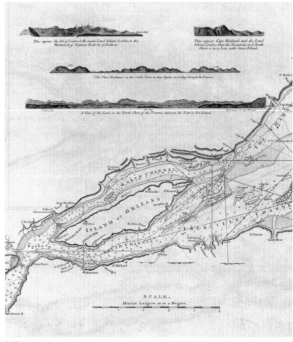

3-10

"Our best seamen or pilots seem to me to be either liars or ignoramuses."

Louis-Joseph de Montcalm

3-10 This chart of the St. Lawrence River is the work of renowned navigator and explorer James Cook. While he was with the Royal Navy, Cook drew his first maps of the St. Lawrence River and Gulf in the fall of 1758. In the winter, he continued his work using surveys done by the French, allowing Vice Admiral Charles Saunders to safely sail up the river in June 1759.

3-11

3-11 Excerpt from the first manifesto written by Major General James Wolfe and nailed to the door of the church in Beaumont, downstream from Lévis.

biggest French offensive of the Siege of Québec. On the night of June 28 and into the early hours of June 29, seven fireships were sent out towards the enemy fleet to set it alight. But the operation was a fiasco: the French fireships were lit too early, and some simply washed up on shore while others were towed away by the British, far from their fleet. It was a crushing defeat for the French, as they had had high hopes for their attack strategy and had invested considerable sums to implement it. British Lieutenant John Knox described the failed attack as a spectacle, noting "They were certainly the grandest fireworks (if I may be allowed to call them that) that can possibly be conceived, every circumstance having contributed to their awful, yet beautiful appearance." A short time later, the military authorities closed the gates to the city for the first time since the beginning of the siege, and Montcalm ordered his men to sleep fully dressed so they would be ready to jump into action.

Cannonballs, Bombs, and Shells

In early July, civilians and soldiers alike were entrenched in the city of Québec and the surroundings, keeping a close eye on the movements of the British troops. While Wolfe soon realized he would be unable to land his troops quickly, he had every intention of launching an offensive to destroy the enemy. In the Point Lévis sector on the south shore of the St. Lawrence, his men were busy building batteries from which to bombard the city across the water, and, before long, four batteries totalling 20 cannons and 13 mortars stood atop the heights. Their destructive arsenal would project cannonballs, bombs, and shells—or fire bombs—causing considerable damage, explosions, and fires.

At the same time, Wolfe set out to push back the French defences in Beauport. On the night of July 8, the British landed a short distance downstream, in Ange-Gardien, and began, according to plan, to set up camp near the Montmorency River opposite the French position. From their location on the shore of the river, they posed a direct threat to the easternmost section of Québec's defensive line. As a result, the Chevalier de Lévis reorganized the French camp in an effort to hold off any British attacks or bombardments.

Meanwhile, the population was troubled by the failed fireship attack and by the British manoeuvres to reinforce their positions at Point Lévis. They openly criticized the French Army's strategy and inaction. The French command continued to dither over whether or not to erect batteries on the south shore, repeatedly delaying an attack to dislodge the enemy and instead ordering the occasional, futile artillery fire. In the end, it was the city's dignitaries—concerned about protecting their property from bombardment—who managed to convince the Marquis de Vaudreuil to take action.

On the evening of July 12, a detachment consisting primarily of militiamen made land upstream from Point Lévis, near the British positions. Their aim was to spike the enemy cannons, rendering them useless, and to dismantle their batteries. The poorly planned expedition quickly fell apart. As the men drew closer to the British camp, confusion and panic broke out among the men, and they turned and fled before the enemy even became aware of their presence. At almost exactly the same time, the batteries began pounding Québec.

Thanks to their superior quality projectiles and gunpowder, the British artillery had an impressive firing range, catching the French command by

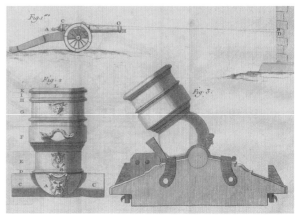

3-12

surprise. The *canonniers* entrenched in the city were helpless in the face of such firepower, plus they had been ordered to ration their ammunition. After the first full night of bombardments, the feeling of terror within the city was palpable. According to Father Jean-Félix Récher, "The British cannonade and bombardment [...] held the entire city in the grips of fear, especially the women and their children, who gathered in large numbers near the Citadel, their tears, lamentations, and prayers continuing unabated as they huddled together and recited their rosaries."

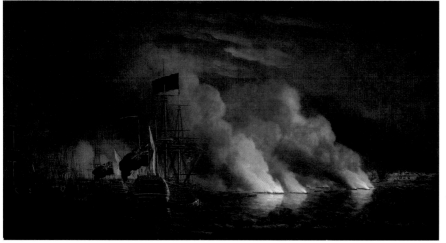

3-13

3-12 In this excerpt from *Traité de l'artillerie*, 1743, the drawing shows a cannon (Figure 1) and mortar (Figure 3).

3-13 During the night of June 28 to 29, the French tried in vain to attack the British fleet using fireships—small boats filled with flammable debris.

The Hôpital général (General hospital) located on the outskirts of the city soon became a refuge. For two full months, Québec was bombarded with cannonballs, bombs, and shells, suffering heavy damage. In addition to numerous public structures, several religious buildings were also either demolished or severely damaged. These included the cathedral, the Jesuit College, and the Notre-Dame-des-Victoires Church. For those inhabitants of the city who hadn't fled in advance of the hostilities, the bombardment only added to the fear and worry caused by rationing and pillage. In fact, robbery had become so widespread that the colonial authorities created a special tribunal tasked with summarily executing anyone caught in possession of stolen goods.

Controlling the River

Despite the shelling of the city, July 1759 was marked by hesitation in the British camp. James Wolfe drafted a series of attack and landing plans, but failed to execute them. Then, in the middle of the month, he ordered a major operation. During the night of July 18, a 50-gun warship, two frigates, and two transport vessels carrying 600 soldiers braved the artillery fire from the Lower Town and sailed to a point just upstream from the city. This seemingly impossible manoeuvre posed another problem for the French strategists. Artillery Officer Montbeillard noted: "This event only heightened our consternation. Had we been mistaken? If the enemy should decide to sail up the river and land somewhere, he could intercept all communication with our food supplies and munitions of war."

By seizing control of the river on both sides of the city, the British forced the French troops to sustain a defensive line stretching nearly 100 kilometres from the Montmorency River to the Batiscan River. Of even greater concern, they were now threatening the city's communications and supply lines. To make matters worse, the recent heavy rains had made travel over land challenging, with the French troops' horses exhausted from struggling through the mud, and their wagons in poor state. With overland routes from Batiscan no longer practicable, transport via the increasingly hazardous river was

3-14

3-14 The lyrics to a song entitled *General Wolfe's Song* appear beneath an engraving depicting the life of the officers in the camps. The men are seated at a table in a tent while two sentries stand guard outside.

3-15

the only available option. Brigadier General James Murray had in fact been ordered to head upstream from Québec with reinforcements to monitor the city's supply lines and destroy the enemy's storehouses and ships along the way. Murray's actions forced Bougainville, his enemy counterpart in the area, to remain on constant high alert.

Montmorency

As July drew to a close, despite his advances upriver from Québec, James Wolfe concluded that the only viable option was to plan a landing along the Beauport coast. The camp that had been set up at the beginning of the month on the left bank of the Montmorency River allowed him to observe and bombard the French positions, as planned. But since the days were passing and the troops were clamouring for action, Wolfe decided to launch a major operation. Concretely, that meant that the grenadiers–soldiers specialized in combat–would have to land at the eastern edge of the French entrenchments and capture

an enemy redoubt located beyond the main defensive line. Once they had seized that advance post, they would use picks and shovels to enlarge and reinforce it. The French Army would then be forced to engage. When the British infantry reinforcements arrived, they would easily vanquish their opponents and would need only to continue their march, cross the St. Charles River, and capture Québec.

The attack was planned for July 30, but with not a breath of wind blowing, any amphibious operation would be impossible, forcing Wolfe to delay until the following day. The postponement only ramped up the tension among the British Army officers. Since the beginning of the siege, relations between the major general and his key officers had been strained. Given their commander's hesitation, many of them had begun to doubt his authority and credibility. While Wolfe was keenly aware of the lack of enthusiasm for his plan of attack, he insisted it go ahead as he had planned it, since his officers had proposed no better alternative.

The attack was finally launched on the morning of July 31. But Wolfe was in for a nasty surprise. As

3-16

3-16 View of the Episcopal Palace, home of the Bishop of Québec, after the British bombardments of 1759.

he was observing the manoeuvres from aboard one of the ships, he realized that the redoubt he had set his sights on was actually closer to the French lines than he had thought, and there was no way his men could withstand the gunfire at that range. He also noticed there was considerable commotion in the enemy camp, but he suspected they were simply disorganized. In actual fact, the French soldiers were reacting to the general alarm sounded by Montcalm by taking up their positions and preparing for battle. As a result, Wolfe decided to alter his strategy, abandoning his relatively simple plan that had consisted of his troops taking up positions and forcing the enemy to attack. Instead, he ordered a massive frontal assault on the entrenchments on the heights.

Wolfe ordered the men stationed at the Montmorency and Point Lévis camps to join the battle. While the enemy movements intensified, Montcalm sought to determine where the landing would take place. In the end, the British landed at the mouth of the Montmorency River. At around 5:30 p.m., the grenadiers, who had grown restless and undisciplined, decided to attack the enemy lines

3-17

3-17 On July 31, 1759, the French Army managed to push back the British, killing 210 and wounding 230, while their own casualties totalled 70 dead and wounded.

without waiting for reinforcements. The French immediately opened fire. The operation was a disaster for the British. The ascent of the escarpment leading to the French lines turned out to be more difficult than originally thought, and, at that same moment, a storm struck, making conditions even more challenging, if not impossible. The heavy rain also soaked the gunpowder, bringing an end to the fight. The attack was a failure, and the British were forced to beat a hasty retreat. By 7:30 p.m., both the storm and the battle were over. The French Army was jubilant!

Wolfe was furious at his men, especially the grenadiers:

The check which the grenadiers met with yesterday will, it is hoped, be a lesson to them for the future. They ought to know that such impetuous, irregular, and unsoldier-like proceeding destroys all order, and makes it impossible for the commander to form any disposition for an attack, and puts it out of the general's power to execute his plan. The grenadiers could not suppose that they alone could beat the French army [...]; the loss however is inconsiderable; and may, if the men shew a proper attention to their officers, be easily repaired when a favourable opportunity offers.

Although Wolfe deemed it inconsequential, the defeat would have a considerable impact on the operations that ensued, dealing a serious blow to the morale of the British troops while further undermining the credibility of the major general. One year earlier, Wolfe had written "I must admit, I'd be delighted to see the Canadian vermin pillaged, plundered and repaid for its cruel actions." As he approached Québec, Wolfe had also expressed his intention, in the event his men had trouble capturing the city, to systematically destroy and ransack the region, leaving behind only desolation. It was no doubt with that sentiment in mind that he came up with his next strategy.

Inflicting Terror

Infuriated by the *Canadiens'* lack of neutrality, James Wolfe decided to carry out the threat that had been

hanging over them since the publication of his manifesto in late June. On July 25, the British announced a series of violent reprisals in a posted notice (in French):

His Excellence [...] has resolved to no longer heed such sentiments of humanity as would assuage the people blinded by their own misery. The Canadiens have proven, through their conduct, unworthy of the advantageous offers he has made them. Consequently, he has issued orders to the commander of his light troops and other officers to advance across the land [...] destroying and ransacking that which they deem fit.

Accordingly, throughout the month of August, the British Army implemented nothing short of a policy of terror. The objective was to encourage the *Canadien* militiamen to desert and to goad Montcalm out of his entrenchments. In addition to stepping up bombardments of the city, Wolfe launched punitive expeditions on both shores of the St. Lawrence, starting with campaigns eastwards along the north shore, all the way to La Malbaie. Then, he gave the order to torch homes and farms, take their inhabitants prisoner, and seize their livestock. A few days later, Wolfe announced his intention to lay waste to the south shore, from Point Lévis to Kamouraska. In a missive to Brigadier General Monckton, he wrote: "It is to very little purpose to withhold the rod, seeing they [the *Canadiens*] are incorrigible."

In describing the reprisals, Assistant Major Jean-Guillaume de La Pause wrote:

Upon his arrival [Wolfe] was tasked with having all of Canada bow beneath the British yoke, yet at present he appears to despair of the success of his endeavour [...] He is ravaging every habitation his troops come across; every home, without exception, has fallen prey to flames, and smoke hangs over the camp from morning to night; from the lower river to the centre of the colony, everything is suffering our enemies' animosity. Québec, although nothing more than a pile of ruins, and a perfect tableau of all the misfortune that war brings to bear, is not enough to quench their hatred.

Brigadier General Townshend expressed the same sentiment, confiding in a letter to his wife: "I

3-18

3-18 Scene of rural life on the south shore of the St. Lawrence River in peacetime. The city of Québec can be seen in the background.

never served so disagreeable a campaign as this. Our unequal force has reduced our operations to a scene of skirmishing, cruelty, and devastation. It is war of the worst shape." In total, nearly 1,400 homes and farms were destroyed, and the crops in their entirety, burned to the ground.

Despite the ransacking, Montcalm stood firm and didn't budge from his positions. But the Marquis was troubled by news he received from the colony's other borders. At Fort Niagara, on Lake Ontario, Pierre Pouchot had been forced to surrender on July 26, 1759, after several days under siege. John Prideaux, who led the besiegers, was killed in the attack and replaced by his second in command, William Johnson, the same man who had overcome and captured Commander Dieskau four years earlier. At the same time, Bourlamaque, who had been tasked with defending the Lake Champlain sector with a reduced army of 3,500 men, had been unable to hold off the charge led by Jeffery Amherst. He abandoned Fort Carillon on July 27, and Fort Saint-Frédéric four days later, before seeking refuge on Île aux Noix on the Richelieu River.

Wolfe Finally Consults his Officers

On August 9, in reaction to these setbacks that left Montreal vulnerable to invasion from the St. Lawrence and Richelieu rivers, Montcalm assigned a detachment of 800 men to the Chevalier de Lévis with orders to make their way to Montreal and to deploy there. As for the city of Québec, he could only hope that, with the season nearing its end, the enemy would be forced to retreat, although he knew that nothing was certain: "It would be surprising if Monsieur Wolfe were to limit himself to fire setting, mayhem, and a single poorly conducted attempt [...] on July 31, with no success to show for it; the man will surely finish with a grand effort, with a thunderclap."

However, while the countryside was being ravaged, the troops besieging Québec, especially those at the front at the Montmorency River, were at a standstill. From the very beginning, there had always been health problems overshadowing James Wolfe's career, namely rheumatism, kidney stones, and lung

3-19

3-19 George Townshend, Third in Command of the Québec Expedition, distinguished himself during the War of the Austrian Succession, notably in the battles at Dettingen (1743), Fontenoy (1745), and Culloden (1746). From 1747 to 1764, he was member of parliament for Norfolk in the House of Commons.

disease. Exhausted by his failed attack of July 31, Wolfe fell ill with a high fever, and was bedridden for several days. He retired to his headquarters on the Beaupré coast, incapable of leading the army's operations and ill inclined to delegate to or consult his military staff. Instead, his staff and troops alike were forced to wait, even though they knew full well that time was running out if they were to keep up the siege. Come winter, Wolfe would be forced to pull his ships from the waters of the St. Lawrence, which would soon ice over, and to shelter his troops from the harsh weather.

"If he gives us battle and we defeat him, Quebec, and probably all Canada, will be our own, which is beyond any advantage we can expect by the Beauport side."

James Wolfe

By late August, Wolfe had regained his health, and finally decided to consult his brigadier generals Monckton, Murray, and Townshend. He proposed three plans of attack to them—all of them simply variations on the Beauport attack—and asked them to determine the best strategy to defeat the enemy. His military staff countered that an attack in the Beauport area was destined to fail, and they instead proposed, together with Vice Admiral Saunders, to attempt an offensive operation in a different part of the city:

We are therefore of opinion that the most probable method of striking an effectual blow is to bring the troops to the south shore, and to carry the operations above the town. If we can establish ourselves on the north shore, the Marquis de Montcalm must fight us on our own terms; we are between him and his provisions, and between him and the army opposing General Amherst. If he gives us battle and we defeat him, Quebec, and probably all Canada, will be our own, which is beyond any advantage we can expect by the Beauport side.

In addition to severing the city's and the French Army's supply line, the operation would have the added effect of preventing the enemy from retreating westwards and finally forcing the Marquis de Montcalm out of his entrenchments to engage in battle. Wolfe eventually accepted the plan, which also had the advantage of exploiting one of the French Army's major weaknesses: the inexperience of the militiamen and the Indigenous warriors when it came to European-style battles on open terrain. An attack in close proximity to the city would also allow him to concentrate his troops and boost their strike force, since he wouldn't have to leave any detachments to protect his base positions. From that moment on, the British Army's actions were coordinated and organized to reflect this plan of attack. □

Insults and Caricatures

During the Siege of Québec, tensions were high between Major General James Wolfe and his military staff consisting of brigadier generals Robert Monckton, James Murray, and George Townshend. From the very first weeks of the campaign, insults flew on all sides. Wolfe discredited the actions of his brigadier generals while the latter accused him of ignoring their opinions. After the July 31 defeat at Montmorency River, the animosity escalated, with the three men openly contesting Wolfe's authority. Townshend was particularly pitiless. He drew a series of caricatures depicting an incompetent and simple-minded major general. In late August, Wolfe finally consulted with his brigadier generals to work out the site of the next landing, but only a few days later, he did an about-face and chose a different site altogether. Monckton, Murray, and Townshend demanded an explanation. In exasperation, Wolfe accused two of them of laziness and the third of being a scoundrel. Several weeks after the victory on the Plains of Abraham where Wolfe perished, Great Britain was gripped by Wolfemania. Some of Townshend's comments and caricatures came back to haunt him, and he was forced to defend his actions and for having mocked a national hero. ■

3-20

3-20 In this caricature, George Townshend depicts James Wolfe as being disrespectful of *Canadien* women.

Chapter Four

THE BATTLE

Feverish Excitement

By the beginning of September, the Siege of Québec had been underway for ten weeks. In the French camp, there were mixed feelings. The threat of famine was becoming more immediate, complicating the defence of the city. Heavy rains had prevented crops in the area from ripening, and the British Army had laid waste to the surrounding countryside and seized the locals' livestock and vegetable harvests. The daily food rations for civilians amounted to one-quarter of a pound of bread, while soldiers were given three-quarters of a pound of bread and half a pound of lard. The remaining quarter-pound of bread the soldiers were denied was made up for by a measure of brandy. As a direct result of the famine, the French Army lost 2,000 militiamen from the heart of the colony when they were forced to go back to their fields to harvest the crops. The government in Montreal had to get wheat to Québec as quickly as possible.

France's military authorities were aware that Wolfe and his men would soon lift the siege because of the lateness of the season, but they knew it was highly unlikely they would retreat before launching a final attack. Despite that, they believed they were safe. A defensive line and the lion's share of the army's troops protected the eastern sector of the north shore of the St. Lawrence, while Bougainville and his troops were guarding the western sector. Between the two, the cliff at Cap Diamant, which towered between 45 and 75 metres high (147 to 246 ft.), formed a natural defence, and only four advance posts guarded it. As he observed the enemy's manoeuvres, the Marquis de Montcalm summed up the situation: "I think Wolfe will act like a player of *tope et tingue* [a French gambling game popular at the time] who, after having played to the left of the *tope*, plays to the right and [then] to the middle. We shall do our best to see him off."

In the early days of September, the British continued to work out the details of their final plan of attack. They stepped up their manoeuvres and carried out diversionary tactics that kept the French Army on high alert. To start with, the camp on the banks of the Montmorency River was evacuated, and the men redeployed to Île d'Orléans and Point Lévis. Then, on September 4, some of the British troops sailed up the St. Lawrence to a point just upstream from the city. The French Army responded by sending detachments and two light cannons to support Bougainville, and relocated its Guyenne battalion to the Plains of Abraham. After spending the night there, the battalion was called back to Beauport.

On September 7, Wolfe and his brigadier generals sailed up the river on a reconnaissance mission to Pointe-aux-Trembles, today known as Neuville. It appears that it was during that excursion that the landing site was selected. The troops were ordered to take their places aboard the transport vessels and warships. Meanwhile, the rain continued to fall. On September 9, the operation had to be called off due

DEBARQUEMENT DE TROUPES CHEZ L'ENNEMI
Ces sortes d'expeditions, sont les plus meurtrieres que la marine peut offrir; quand le rivage ou l'on veut descendre; est bien defendu: l'usage ordinaire dans ces sortes d'attaques est d'emvoier d'abord des Fregattes, ou Prames A, canoner les Batteries, ou retranchements s'il y en a, afin d'en chasser l'ennemi ou du moins, essayer de l'ebranler; on jette aussi des bombes, aux environs du Rivage, afin d'empecher autant qu'il est possible, à aucuns corps de troupes d'approcher, pour s'opposer à la descente. C'est à la faveur de cette canonade, que les chaloupes B, portent à terre les soldats et ustancil es necessaires pour former un retranchan; s'il en est besoin: quand le rivage n'est pas assez étendu pour permettre a toutes les chaloupes d'y aborder de front, elles s'approchent a la file de la1re C, et on descend, en passant de l'une dans l'autre; on fait aussi quelquefois des attaques fausses, ou réelles suivant le dessein que l'on a, de partager les forces de l'ennemi, ou de s'emparer à revers, des batteries qui peuvent nuire au debarquement, Ces expeditions sont ordinairement protegées par de gros Vaisseaux. D

4-1

---

to the heavy precipitation. The conditions were so bad that no military operations could be undertaken, and the health of the men crowded onto the ships was deemed in jeopardy.

As a result, the troops were given the order to land on the south shore, at Saint-Nicolas, and to remain ready to embark. Major General Wolfe was dismayed by the situation: "The weather has been extremely unfavourable for a day or two, so that we have been inactive. I am so far recovered as to do business, but my constitution is entirely ruined, without the consolation of having done any considerable service to the State, or without any prospect of it."

Anse au Foulon

Forced into inactivity, Wolfe and a few officers decided to explore the shoreline once again. As one of the men, James Thompson, observed:

> *The Bank which runs along the Shore is very steep and woody, and [...] the French themselves, that they had then only a single Pickett to defend it. This Pickett [...] was encamped upon the Bank, near the top of a narrow winding path which runs up from the shore. This path*

"These circumstances, joined to the distance of the place from succors, seemed to promise a fair chance of success."

James Thompson

4-1 In his collection of essays *Recueil des différents vaisseaux qui servent à la guerre*, naval engineer Nicolas-Marie Ozanne discusses the manoeuvres related to the attack and defence of ports. In describing landings, he writes "These kinds of expeditions are the deadliest that the Navy can offer."

was broken up by the Enemy themselves, and barricaded with an abbatis; but about two hundred yards to the right, there appeared to be a slope in the bank which it was thought might answer to purpose. These circumstances, joined to the distance of the place from succors, seemed to promise a fair chance of success.

On September 10, Wolfe decided to change the plan of attack and execute the landing at a point closer to the city than that agreed on with his military staff. He opted instead to land at Anse au Foulon, on the north shore of the St. Lawrence, about a kilometre and a half (one mile) from the ramparts of Québec. However, the new site comprised its share of challenges: a cliff to be scaled, positioned midway between Montcalm's troops in Beauport and Bougainville's troops in Cap-Rouge, the difficulty of beating a retreat if need be, and the impossibility of using the artillery. What's more, any attack hoping to escape the enemy's notice would have to take place under cover of night. On the up side, landing at Anse au Foulon would allow Wolfe to easily regroup his men who were stationed on Île d'Orléans and at Point Lévis, to align all his troops near the city and, consequently, to finally flush the Marquis de Montcalm from his entrenchments.

However, Wolfe's plan did not sit well with his military staff and the officers of the Royal Navy, who all deemed it too risky. In hindsight, Rear Admiral Charles Holmes summed up their concerns: "For the distance of the landing Place; the impetuosity of the Tide; the darkness of the Night; & the great Chance of exactly hitting the very Spot intended, without discovery or alarm, made the whole extremely difficult." The brigadier generals demanded more details about the operation. Alone in his conviction, Wolfe ignored Murray and Townshend, responding only to Monckton: "I had the honour to inform You to day, that it is my duty to attack, the French Army, to the best of my knowledge, & abilities, I have fix'd upon that spot, where we can act with the most force, & are most likely to succeed, if I am mistaken, I am sorry for it; & must be answerable to his Majesty & the Publick for the consequences."

Meanwhile in the French camp, all the regiments were on high alert, ready to rush to the defence of the sectors to the east and west of Québec. Montbeillard confidently wrote: "Monsieur le Marquis de Montcalm and I wandered at length along the entrenchments, and the more I examined them, the more I was persuaded that the enemy would not attack them. The lines and redoubts had

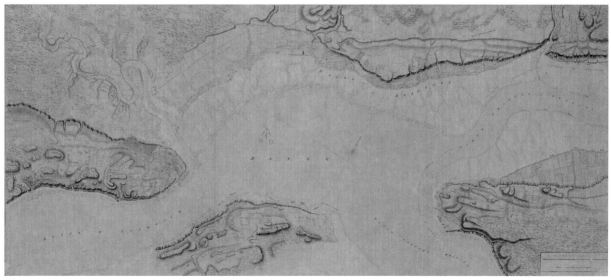

4-2

been repaired, and I felt that our troops, entrenched as they were, would be invincible."

The Approach

On September 12 at nine p.m., with their ships at anchor just off Saint-Nicolas, the British soldiers making up the advance guard of the troops took their places aboard eight landing craft that were moored next to the *Sutherland* warship and awaited the signal. Since the soldiers had been forced to wait for hours, they were given an extra ration of hot water spiked with rum. According to an entry in the logbook of one of the ships taking part in the operation, conditions were ideal: "Fine weather, the night calm, and silence over all."

The role of the landing craft was to transport the advance guard and then ferry the troops from the ships to the shore. The boats had been designed and built the year before in order to enhance the safety and speed of amphibious operations. They were a little over nine metres (29 feet) in length and 3 metres (9 feet) wide, with a draft of barely 60 centimetres (less than 2 feet). The landing craft were powered by sixteen oarsmen who served as a human shield for the 50 soldiers they carried. Some 22 other boats, including barges, rowboats, and cutters, assisted them in the operation. Wolfe estimated their average speed at 2.4 knots, and calculated that it would take them two hours to cover the distance between the ships and Anse au Foulon, some twenty kilometres (12½ miles) downstream.

The Anse au Foulon sector was guarded by two French Army advance posts. To the west, on the Samos Battery, stood three 24-pounder cannons and one 13-inch mortar. Thirty soldiers from the Languedoc Regiment under Captain François Douglas manned the battery. To the east, separated from the Samos Battery by two gullies, a detachment of 100 militiamen and soldiers from the Marine troops were camped 55 metres (180 feet) above the river's edge. These men were under the orders of Captain Louis de Vergor, signatory of the capitulation of Fort Gaspareaux in 1755. One part of the detachment formed a chain of sentinels along the escarpment, while the other part kept watch over

4-3

4-4 Depiction of the Samos Battery. A battery usually consists of a parapet of gabions (interwoven branches filled in with dirt) and platforms on which stand pieces of artillery and magazines (small dugouts built to house ammunition). Inside the battery, the pieces of artillery are usually laid out at intervals of about five metres (16 feet) and fired through embrasures, or openings, in the parapet wall.

the trench and the abattis blocking the path leading from Anse au Foulon to the top of the cliffs of Cap Diamant.

At ten o'clock, the moon began to rise. The light from it was dim, as it was already in its last quarter. One hour later, the British Army began to employ diversionary tactics. The *Sutherland* sailed upriver to Cap-Rouge, where the plan was to keep Bougainville's troops occupied, while most of the fleet shuttled back and forth in front of Beauport and the mouth of the St. Charles River. The French authorities were especially nervous about movement in the latter sector. Meanwhile, the artillery at Point Lévis stepped up its shelling of Québec. At two o'clock in the morning, two lanterns were lit on the main mast of the *Sutherland*: the signal had been given!

The advance guard made up of light infantry of about 400 men immediately cast off. Their mission was to precede the rest of the troops and neutralize the French advance posts defending Anse au Foulon, so as to secure the main landing. The men took advantage of the tide to drift into shore in complete silence. The rest of the first wave of troops followed close behind and, at regular intervals, the ships carrying cannons, ammunition, and supplies, as well as the second and third wave of troops.

At three o'clock, just as the British advance guard reached Sillery and met up with the *Hunter*,

the men were told that a French supply convoy was on its way. Indeed, nineteen riverboats had reached Cap-Rouge and were preparing to undertake the final section towards Québec. The advance posts defending the city were therefore on the lookout for the convoy. What they didn't know was that it had been cancelled, and the message hadn't been passed on to the troops. Hugging the north shore, the British boats were quickly hailed by the French sentinels. In impeccable French, a captain from the 78th Highlanders Regiment replied that they were bearing the eagerly-awaited supplies, and they were allowed to continue on their way. But when they saw the boats veering instead towards Anse au Foulon, the sentinels immediately opened fire.

Tackling the Cliff

Wolfe's plan called for his troops to land upstream from Anse au Foulon and execute a direct attack on the barricaded and entrenched path. However, the tide carried the boats east beyond the planned landing site. At 4:07 a.m., after clambering over the bow of their boat onto the shore, a detachment of 24 volunteers commanded by Captain William DeLaune ran to their left towards the path.

At the head of the light infantry, Lieutenant Colonel William Howe contemplated the dark and

4-4

foreboding cliff towering before him, concluding that it was not merely steep, but practically vertical. It was an impressive sight. One of the soldiers noted: "If the General should attempt to ascend the rock, it is a work of much labour and difficulty, if at all practicable; and should our troops perform this difficult undertaking, I shall for the future think little of Hanibal's leading an army over the Alps; the rock is almost steep, and the summit seems to me inaccessible to an army."

Since time was of the essence, and his troops were already the target of sniper fire, Howe ordered his men to scale the cliff without delay. The ground was covered with shale fragments which, after days of rain, were wet and slippery, complicating their efforts. The men had no choice but to clamber up the slope, gripping on to the roots and tree branches clinging to the escarpment as they went.

As they ascended the cliff, they were spotted by a soldier, but one of the British soldiers who spoke French managed to convince him that their detachment was on the same side. The officer ordered the man back to his sentry post and to call off the sentinels' watch. The way was now free all the way up to the post defended by Captain Vergor. Meanwhile, the first wave of troops, which included James Wolfe, landed at Anse au Foulon, where they were fired on by French soldiers posted at the top of the cliff, where the battle had already begun.

Surprise Attack

Caught off guard by an attack from the rear, Vergor ordered his troops to turn and fight, but in the space of only a few minutes, he suffered wounds to his hand and leg. Half of his men were taken prisoner, while the

4-5

"The rock is almost steep, and the summit seems to me inaccessible to an army."

British soldier

rest attempted to flee to Québec. With the British in pursuit, many ended up surrendering, while a few managed to escape. It was four thirty in the morning.

Further west, alerted by the sound of scattered gunshots, the Samos Battery jumped into action, pounding the British boats with cannonfire. A detachment of grenadiers promptly began attacking from the rear. At the orders of Captain François Douglas, most of the soldiers manning the battery abandoned their cannons for muskets. During the skirmish, only one 24-pounder cannon managed to fire against the British. The grenadiers were soon joined by a detachment of light infantry, and the pressure on Douglas and his men grew untenable, although before they could fall to defeat, they spiked their cannons and mortar and beat a retreat.

After neutralizing Vergor's camp, Howe and his men rushed to the path on the promontory to demolish the abattis and bridge the trench that was blocking access to it. There they ran into DeLaune and his detachment, who had opted to ascend via the path. Wolfe was immediately informed of the success of his advance guard and went to join his men to reconnoitre the terrain. For his own safety, he donned a discreet uniform consisting of a red coat, waistcoat, and breeches, with no military regalia, and he swapped his sword for a rifle and bayonet. Reassured, he ordered the landing to continue.

The sound of gunfire could now be heard from inside the walls of Québec. As acting commander of the garrison, since Ramezay had been hospitalized with the flu, Lieutenant Colonel Félicien de Bernetz was informed of the attack by a messenger who had come from Vergor's camp. He immediately ordered a cannon to be fired to alert the Beauport camp and petitioned the governor general to send in reinforcements. From his camp, Vaudreuil wrote to Bougainville, who was still in Cap-Rouge, informing him of the landing at Anse au Foulon. Montreuil, the aide-major general posted at the bridge over the St. Charles River, was also alerted. Around half-past five, he deployed two detachments from the Guyenne Regiment to the Plains of Abraham. At Camp de la Canardière, between the St. Charles River and Beauport, Montbeillard was, in turn, informed of the developments by a member of the militia: "This *Canadien* told us with the fervour of

4-6

4-6 Grenadiers scaling the cliff. Easily distinguished by their mitre hats, they formed a special unit that was created by Wolfe in Louisbourg in preparation for the expedition against Québec.

4-7

4-7 This watercolour by George Heriot depicts the Plains of Abraham circa 1795. With their vastness and their proximity to the gates of the city of Québec, the Plains held great strategic importance.

4-8 With his 1909 portrayal of the Battle of the Plains of Abraham, Québec painter Charles Huot was the first artist to depict the battle from the point of view of the French Army.

undisputed fear that he was the only one to have escaped and that the enemy was on the heights. We well knew the difficulties of breaking through at that point, poorly defended though it was, and we did not believe a word of the account of a man whose head, we believed, had been turned by fear." A few kilometres to the east, Montcalm learned of the landing a short while later.

At the same time, the British were making their way up the path that allowed them to ascend the cliff with their muskets in hand (a weapon superior to that of the French in terms of range and firing frequency), enough ammunition for 70 shots, two days of rations, as well as flasks of water and rum. The men also managed to haul two bronze, six-pounder field cannons up the cliff. On the river, there was a flurry of activity as boats ferried back and forth. The wounded were taken to a field hospital set up in a church at Point Lévis, while the troops were carried from the transport ships to the north shore. Approximately 4,400 British troops came ashore at Anse au Foulon on the morning of September 13.

The Battlefield

Once he reached the top of the promontory, James Wolfe found himself in a wooded area. Despite the forest cover, he managed to form his lines, back to the river, right flank facing the city, left flank facing Sillery. Clearly, he feared an imminent attack from the French Army, but since it didn't materialize, the major general reconnoitred the terrain to find an open area that would be long enough to assemble his men out of range of enemy fire, wide enough to allow him to position them in formation, and flat enough to avoid his troops becoming dispersed during the manoeuvre. He summoned engineer and cartographer Samuel Holland, who was familiar with the terrain, to accompany him.

The two men scouted out the escarpment towards the city until the forest grew sparser, and there they came upon a vast terrain known as the Plains of Abraham. The easternmost part was relatively open, and the ground was covered in some areas with meadow grass and white clover, and in others with wheat. One drawback, however, was that the area was at the base of a hill known as Buttes à Neveu, a position of strength that Wolfe would concede to the French Army since, to launch an attack, the French would have to traverse a terrain described by the Chevalier de Lévis as "difficult, encumbered, uneven, and covered with thickets in parts." At six o'clock that morning, Wolfe ordered his troops to fall into line, just as it began to rain.

When news of the landing made its way to the city, Bernetz sent a detachment of militiamen and Indigenous warriors as reinforcements to Anse au Foulon, but it was too late, as the advance posts had already been taken. The reinforcements headed instead to the Plains of Abraham, where they joined up with the Guyenne Regiment, which had been deployed there by Montreuil. Together, they opened fire on the British in an attempt to prevent the enemy from falling into formation. But their efforts were in vain. With the arrival of the second and third wave of troops, the British line formed, growing bigger by the minute. Of the 4,400 men who landed at Anse au Foulon, 2,100 formed the firing line, while the remaining 2,300 protected the flanks north and south of the line, as well as the landing area.

In order to cover as large an area as possible, James Wolfe positioned his men in two long lines instead of the usual three. In fact, only the 78th Highlanders Regiment was aligned in the traditional manner. One six-pounder cannon was set up at either end of

4-8

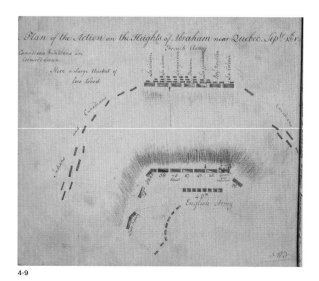

4-9

the line, which stretched some 800 to 900 metres (2,600 to 2,900 feet). To maximize their firing power, Wolfe ordered his men to load their muskets with two balls and to wait until the enemy was within 35 metres (115 feet) before firing.

A few days earlier, Montbeillard had written: "To be defeated is the common misfortune of the weaker; but to be taken by surprise is the height of misfortune." His words would prove to be prescient. When Montcalm was told of the landing, his regular troops and militiamen were already on the march or engaged in battle, positioned in lines on Buttes à Neveu. At seven o'clock, he gave the order for the troops in Beauport to march to the Plains of Abraham, a distance of about six kilometres (3¾ miles). By eight o'clock, he was on the battlefield himself, and by half past nine, all the French units had joined him.

The Marquis de Montcalm opted to deploy his regiments in three lines. The militiamen were incorporated in the middle line, to keep them in formation. Together they formed a line that, like the British line, stretched out over some 800 to 900 metres. Detachments from the Marine troops and militia were posted at either end, in the wooded area, while other militiamen and the Indigenous warriors kept up fire on the British flanks. Montcalm was at the head of an army of 3,500 men, only half of whom were trained soldiers. Not including the

troops assigned to the flanks, the French firing line was essentially equivalent to the British line (i.e., approximately 2,000 men). On the battlefield, the French Army also had five pieces of artillery (twelve-, six-, and four-pounder cannons).

The Battle

With less than 500 metres (1,640 feet) separating his men from the British Army, Montcalm analyzed the situation: "We cannot avoid action; the enemy is entrenched, he already has two pieces of cannons. If we give him time to establish himself, we shall never be able to attack him with the sort of troops we have. [...] Is it possible that Bougainville doesn't hear all that noise?" Alerted earlier by Vaudreuil, the captain should have already made his way to the battlefield from Cap-Rouge. To the marquis's mind, retreating behind the city walls was not an option, as he feared the fortifications would be unable to withstand a siege. His only choice therefore was to launch an attack.

At around ten o'clock, the rain stopped. Fearing the British Army would become further entrenched, Montcalm gave the order to attack, without waiting for Bougainville and his men. Leaving its advantageous position on the hill, the French Army advanced too quickly, the men struggling to make their way around and over the terrain's natural obstacles. They soon broke ranks and the formation fell apart, with some troops advancing quickly and others lagging behind, some veering right, others going left, and those in the middle left on their own. When they got to within 120 metres (393 feet) of the British line, the men stopped and prepared to open fire. Without awaiting their orders, the militia in the second line and the soldiers in the third line began to shoot, then dropped to the ground to reload their muskets. Their fire, ineffective at that range, caused only minor injuries, and the fact they were suddenly prone only served to create further disorder within the French ranks. Nevertheless, the French soldiers continued to advance, attempting to regroup as they went.

The disciplined British soldiers followed their commander's orders and allowed the enemy to draw closer before firing. When the French Army got to

4-10

4-9 This map shows the positions
of the French and British armies
prior to the battle on September
13, 1759. It is an excerpt from
a journal kept by an officer of
the British Army's 35th infantry
regiment, quite possibly Lieutenant
Colonel Henry Fletcher.

4-11

"Nothing [...] could stop the men fleeing; they had fallen prey to a terror without parallel."

Pierre Marcel

4-11 This excerpt from *Encyclopédie, ou Dictionnaire raisonné des sciences, des arts et des métiers* depicts a series of infantry exercises, including how to load a musket, take aim, and fire.

within 90 metres (295 feet), Wolfe's men began to advance in steady formation. The platoons began shooting and exchanging crossfire. As the French drew nearer, the British artillerymen traded their grapeshot for musket balls. When the two armies were within 35 metres (114 feet) of each other, they stopped and faced off, each side waiting for the other to fire first. The first salvo came from the French side. The British Army immediately responded with a devastating volley that had the effect of "a single cannon-shot," according to Lieutenant John Knox. The first line of the French Army was decimated, and the two others, in total disarray.

The French troops attempted to counterattack, but were unsuccessful. The British soldiers advanced a few paces to escape the thick smoke produced by their own musket fire and fired off another salvo. In the French ranks, the troops decided to beat a retreat, and the soldiers fled to the city, with the British in pursuit, their bayonets mounted on their muskets. According to Pierre Marcel, Montcalm's aide-de-camp, "Nothing [...] could stop the men fleeing; they had fallen prey to a terror without parallel."

The Retreat

The *Canadien* militiamen posted on the flanks kept up their fire, managing to slow the British charge led by the Highlanders and allowing the French Army to retreat to the city. When he arrived on the scene, Vaudreuil attempted in vain to reorganize the troops. But around noon, the hostilities ended when the *Canadiens* and the Indigenous warriors could no longer hold off the enemy fire, the British charge had been pushed back by the artillery at the mouth of the St. Charles River, and most of the French troops had sought refuge at the Beauport camp. Delayed by a skirmish with a British platoon three kilometres from the battlefield, Bougainville didn't reach the site until the battle was already over. He had little choice but to retreat. The actual battle on the Plains Abraham had lasted less than thirty minutes. However, approximately eight hours had passed between the first exchange of gunfire at the Vergor camp and the final cannonade at the mouth of the St. Charles River.

The battlefield was a scene of carnage, the ground littered with bodies. James Wolfe had suffered a

A National Hero

On September 13, 1759, Major General James Wolfe was mortally wounded by a shot to the chest. In the hours that followed, his body was embalmed and placed in a coffin. On September 18, the day marking the surrender of Québec, his remains were stowed aboard the *Royal William*, which set sail for England. The ship arrived in Portsmouth on November 17. To the sound of cannon fire and bells, the coffin was laid on a horse-drawn hearse and the procession set out for London. All along the route, the cortege was greeted by thousands of people. Three days later, James Wolfe was buried in his family's vault in the Greenwich cemetery.

The wave of patriotism inspired by the British victory on the Plains of Abraham quickly elevated James Wolfe to the rank of national hero. He became the very incarnation of the courageous officer who made the ultimate sacrifice to expand the British Empire. Poems, songs, and illustrations hailed his victory and perpetuated his memory. In 1770, American painter Benjamin West produced an iconic work entitled *The Death of General Wolfe*. Although his work garnered accolades, it was met with reticence in academic circles, as the figures it depicted wore contemporary dress rather than the vintage garments prescribed by the conventions of historical paintings at the time. West was subsequently invited to serve in the court of King George III. His painting inspired a number of artists, including François-Louis-Joseph Watteau, who painted a similar canvas in 1783, *La Mort de Montcalm*. ∎

4-12

4-12 This sketch is the only remaining study of Benjamin West's work. In it, the artist has set out the figures and the dramatic lighting of the scene in a manner reminiscent of the *Lamentation of Christ*. James Wolfe lies dying, his eyes heavenward, surrounded by his brothers in arms. West took a number of creative liberties, his goal being not to depict the historic truth, but rather to portray Wolfe's noble sacrifice.

wound to his right wrist at the beginning of the battle, and was subsequently shot beneath the navel and in the chest, the final projectile perforating his right lung. The major general was carried off the field by his men and died a short time later. At eleven o'clock, his body was taken aboard a ship that was bound for England a few days later. Meanwhile, the Marquis de Montcalm had suffered wounds to his arm and thigh during the battle. As he was retreating to the city, he was shot through from behind. With the help of his men, he entered the gates of the city and was taken to the home of surgeon Arnoux. The French Army estimated its losses at 150 dead, 193 wounded, and 370 taken prisoner, while the British counted 61 dead and 603 wounded.

That afternoon, the Marquis de Vaudreuil went to Montcalm's deathbed to seek his counsel. The general gave him three options: launch another attack, retreat to the mouth of the Jacques-Cartier River some fifty kilometres (31 miles) west of the ramparts, or capitulate in the name of the entire colony. In a letter to the Chevalier de Lévis, who was still in Montreal, Vaudreuil summed up his opinion:

Firstly, we are in no condition to take our revenge as soon as this evening; our army is too disheartened [...], if we wait until tomorrow, the enemy shall be entrenched in a position it will be impossible to attack. Second, I cannot and shall never agree to capitulate on behalf of the entire colony. Third, our retreat is therefore indispensable, all the more so as we are forced by our own subsistence. Upon full consideration of the above, I shall leave this evening with the remnants of the army to take up position at Jacques-Cartier [...].

At six o'clock, after a council of war, his decision came into force.

Meanwhile, the British Army continued to dig in around the city gates and seized the Hôpital général. During the night of September 13, they proceeded to spike the French batteries. As for the troops who had withdrawn to the Beauport camp, they received the order to break camp in silence and to take with them as many musket balls and as much gunpowder as they could carry, as well as food for four days. The march to the Jacques-Cartier River began in a disorderly fashion, with the militiamen taking advantage of the retreat to return to their homes. In the early hours of September 14, the Marquis de Montcalm succumbed to his injuries. He was buried the same day in a bomb crater beneath the Ursuline Chapel. □

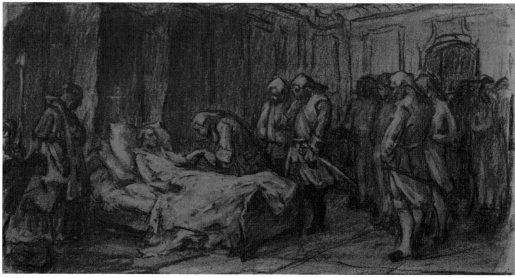

4-13

4-14

4-13 Before painting *La Mort de Montcalm*, Marc-Aurèle de Foy Suzor-Côté did a series of preparatory studies. This one shows Montcalm lying on his deathbed, surrounded by military and religious figures, perhaps symbolizing the "death" of the colony and Catholicism, respectively.

4-14 "In the year one thousand seven hundred and fifty-nine, on the fourteenth of the month of September, was interred in the Church of the Ursuline Nuns of Québec the high and almighty Lord Louis-Joseph Marquis de Montcalm, Lieutenant General of the King's armies, Commander of the Royal and Military Order of Saint-Louis, Commander in Chief of the Land Troops in North America, who did perish from his wounds suffered in battle the previous day, comforted by the Sacraments he received with much piety and Religion."

Chapter Five

WINTER

Capitulation

The two armies were in turmoil following the September 13 battle. The French camp, in particular, was in utter chaos, with the troops regrouped at the mouth of the Jacques-Cartier River, while Ramezay, who had been discharged from hospital, was in command of the garrison that had retreated to Québec, its resources severely depleted. On September 15, the Chevalier de Lévis was informed of the defeat of the French Army on the Plains of Abraham and of the mortal wounds the Marquis de Montcalm had suffered. As Montcalm's successor as commander of the regular troops, the Chevalier de Lévis received the order to leave Montreal and join Vaudreuil at the Jacques-Cartier River.

Having taken over command of the British Army in the wake of James Wolfe's death, and in light of the wounds sustained on the battlefield by Second in Command Robert Monckton, Brigadier General George Townshend set about fortifying the entrenchments at the city gates. While some troops unloaded supplies and pieces of artillery, others carried out fortification work, including erecting redoubts and batteries. The besiegers' main goal was to begin bombarding the city as soon as possible from the heights of the Buttes à Neveu.

Isolated and exhausted, the garrison attempted a show of resistance, but managed little more than to slow the enemy's building efforts. With food in short supply for the 6,000 mouths he needed to

5-1

5-1 Summary of the remaining food provisions available to sustain the Québec garrison, dated September 15, 1759.

feed, Ramezay hoped desperately the rest of the French Army would provide relief. On September 15, he received a request from the city's dignitaries beseeching him to negotiate the terms of capitulation so as to save the population from famine and from an enemy capable of "sacrificing, without distinction for standing, age, or gender, anyone who crossed their path."

Ramezay convened his council of war, which consisted of the senior officers of the garrison's land and Marine troops, and informed them of Vaudreuil's instructions stipulating that "they must not wait until the enemy take them by assault; thus, once their provisions have been exhausted, they shall hoist the white flag and send the garrison's most capable and intelligent officer to propose capitulation." Only Jacau de Fiedmont, Commander of the Artillery, refused to surrender, instead suggesting that the French "further reduce the rations, and persevere in defending the place to the very last extremity." As far as the others were concerned, the shortage of food and the faint hope of receiving any relief justified the decision to capitulate under the most honourable of terms. However, a missive from Vaudreuil insisting that Ramezay hold out until reinforcements arrived spurred him to postpone his decision.

On September 16, Ramezay was informed that most of the French troops were still at the mouth

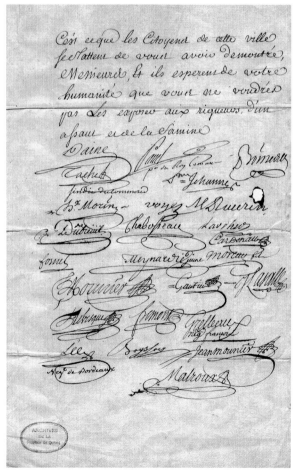

5-2

5-2 Signatures of the dignitaries who, on September 15, 1759, implored Jean-Baptiste-Nicolas-Roch de Ramezay, Commander of the Québec Garrison, to avoid exposing the city's residents to "the rigours of an attack and to famine" by capitulating.

A Shower of Bombs

On September 2, 1759, George Williamson, commander of the British artillery, claimed to have fired on Québec a total of 2,498 thirteen-inch mortar shells, 1,920 ten-inch mortar shells, 283 thirteen-inch carcass projectiles, 93 ten-inch carcass projectiles, 11,500 twenty-four-pounder round shots, and 1,589 thirty-two-pounder round shots. At the end of the Battle of the Plains of Abraham, Québec's priest, Father Jean-Félix Récher, wrote: "During the siege, the English fired '40 et quelques mille coups de canon' and nearly ten thousand bombs." ■

5-3

5-3 Inside of the Récollets Church after the British bombardments in 1759.

of the Jacques-Cartier River, where Vaudreuil was attempting to organize two convoys to support the garrison: one made up of a hundred or so cavalrymen each carrying a sack of "biscuit" and another of 600 soldiers also carrying food supplies. On the 17th, the Chevalier de Lévis arrived from Montreal. He was determined to reach Québec in time to evacuate the garrison and destroy what was left of the city so the British couldn't spend the winter there. However, given the scarcity of food, the troops' departure was delayed until the next morning. Only the two convoys set out for Québec.

Meanwhile, Ramezay was concerned that the enemy manoeuvres being reported on the river and on land were a sign another attack was imminent. At around eleven o'clock in the morning, fearing reinforcements would never arrive, he hoisted the parliamentary flag, much to the surprise of the British, whose batteries would not yet be operational for another two or three days. In fact, Ramezay had taken a gamble to wait for reinforcements while undertaking negotiations to surrender.

At four in the afternoon, Lieutenant Joannes was dispatched to negotiate with Townshend, with orders to "stall for time." However, just before midnight, despite the arrival of the first convoy of cavalrymen, Ramezay brought the negotiations to a close. Doubtful of the ability of the reinforcements to push back the British, and hoping to avoid a second attack, he agreed to capitulate. Townshend, in turn, agreed to grant the honours of war to the French garrison. The men would be allowed to march out of the city bearing their arms and flags, but would not be able to join the army and "shall be embarked as conveniently as possible, to be sent to the first port in France." The Articles of the Capitulation of Québec were signed at eight o'clock in the morning on September 18. Upon hearing the news, Bougainville wrote: "The English have only walls, and the colony still belongs to the King." Those were fighting words.

Taking Possession of the City

At around half past three on the afternoon of September 18, British battalions and an artillery detachment took possession of the city, namely its gates and government buildings, and secured the sites. They wasted no time hoisting the Union Jack and seizing the meagre rations of food and ammunition that had been left behind. During the night, a group of French and *Canadien* soldiers, sailors, and militiamen managed to flee the city and make their way back to join the French troops. The next day, the rest of the British troops entered the devastated city. According to Lieutenant John Knox, "The havoc is not to be conceived. Such houses as are standing are perforated by our shot, more and less; and the low town is so great a ruin that its streets are almost impassable."

While marching towards the city with his reinforcements, Lévis learned, with consternation, of the surrender. In reaction to the news, he wrote: "This news, which rendered all of my actions meaningless, afflicted me immensely. It is astonishing to surrender a place without it being either attacked or invaded." Ramezay's decision caused an outcry among the French officers. But all the troops could do was retreat back to the Jacques-Cartier River once again, where Lévis had a fort erected that would become the army's bridgehead.

On September 20, the Québec garrison embarked aboard four ships, which only actually set sail for France one month later. In addition to the French soldiers were a handful of civilians who, uncertain of what lay in store for them, preferred to leave the colony. As for the city's *habitants* who stayed behind, they were left few options by Monckton, who had resumed his role as commander: "They may return to their parishes and take possession of their lands,

"The English have only walls, and the colony still belongs to the King."

Louis-Antoine de Bougainville

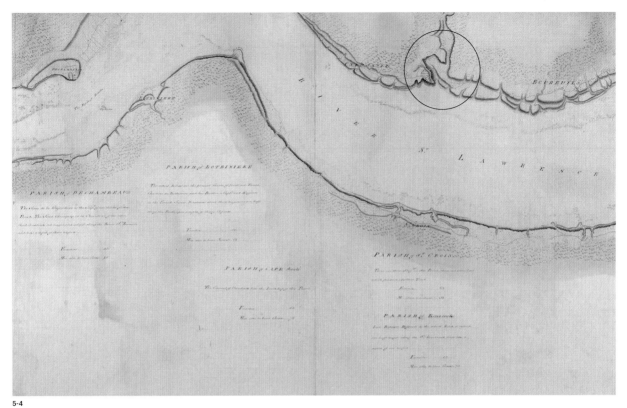

5-4

5-5

5-4 After the defeat of September 13, 1759, Lévis ordered the building of Fort Jacques-Cartier at the mouth of the river of the same name. From September to December of that year, some 200 men were put to work to erect the fort.

5-5 Robert Monckton, Second in Command in the campaign against Québec, headed up the right wing of the British Army on September 13, 1759. He suffered a chest wound during the battle.

Taking an Oath
of Allegiance

"I solemnly promise and swear before God that I will be faithful to his Britannic Majesty King George the Second, that I will not take up arms against him, and that I will not give any intelligence to his enemies who might in any way injure him." It was in accordance with these terms that the *habitants* of Québec and the surrounding parishes swore an oath of allegiance, in the fall of 1759, to the monarch of Great Britain and pledged to the occupying army their good conduct. ■

5-6

homes, and belongings, harvest their crops, enjoy their religion without let or hindrance on the part of the English [...] provided that they, for their part, hand over their arms, swear an oath of allegiance, and stay tranquilly in their homes." Exhausted, starving, and fearful, the population had no other choice but to comply.

Fortifying and Controlling

With the help of George Townshend, Robert Monckton spent the first few days following the surrender arranging the resupply of the British garrison and re-establishing order in the ranks. To ensure the well-being of his troops, his priority was to secure the basic necessities such as food, water, medicine, and fuel. And since winter was approaching, a large supply of wood was needed, so Monckton ordered his men to gather anything they could from the remains of the destroyed houses, and sent out teams on wood-cutting expeditions. He also set about restoring discipline among the men, by rewarding those who denounced others and implementing an elaborate system of patrols and control points.

Meanwhile, Charles Saunders and the Royal Navy busied themselves unloading part of the material required for the garrison. Once this mission was accomplished, since he couldn't leave his large ships on the St. Lawrence during the winter, the vice admiral left two sloops of war and three schooners close to the city and deployed the rest with a detachment to Halifax under the command of Navy Officer Alexander Colvill, who had orders to return to Québec as early as possible in the spring.

On October 18, Townshend embarked with Saunders and his fleet, and they set sail for Great Britain, where news had just arrived of the British victory of September 13. On the other side of the Atlantic, William Pitt was ecstatic, and the British people celebrated. The Conquest of Québec, which came on the heels of the series of victories on lakes Champlain and Ontario, was the crowning event of what became known as a miraculous year, or the *Annus Mirabilis*. In France, the news was published in the November 3 issue of the *Gazette*, and garnered little reaction.

Monckton was the next to leave Québec, two weeks later, however he was headed to New York. His successor, Brigadier General James Murray,

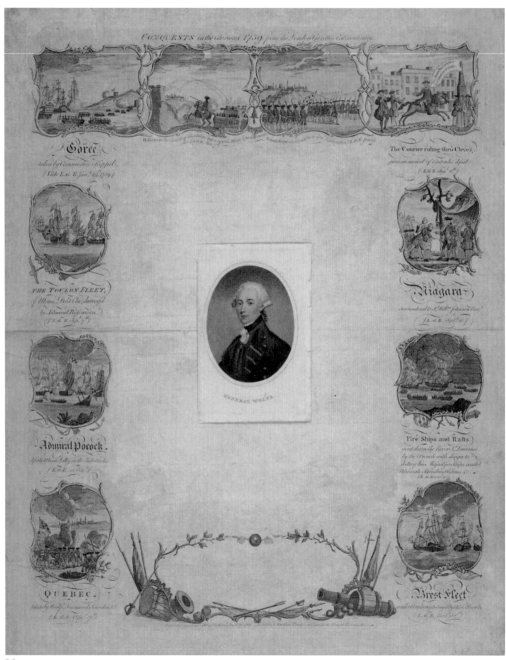

5-8

5-9

was appointed governor of the Québec garrison. Although winter was too imminent for the Chevalier de Lévis to attempt to retake the capital in the short term, Murray was convinced it was only a matter of time. His immediate priority was to reinforce the city's fortifications. He had a defence line erected on the promontory consisting of seven blockhouses, among other structures, and had his men reinforce the heights of Cap-Rouge as well as the churches of Sainte-Foy and Ancienne-Lorette with cannons.

Despite being kept busy with all these tasks, the British troops nevertheless felt a sense of isolation. Tensions ran high in the ranks, as borne out by a number of acts of indiscipline. There were far more deserters than would usually be expected. To Murray's mind, "the plundering kind of War which had been carried on this last Campaign had so Debauched the Soldier, that there was no putting a stop to these without very severe punishment," which is why he promised a reward to anyone who had information that would lead to the apprehension of a deserter. With regard to the widespread scourge of thievery and drunkenness, he attempted to put an end to it with corporal punishment, like floggings.

Murray also sought to exert control over the local population, as the people were badly shaken and troubled by the recent events. To start with, in mid-October, he introduced a new order requiring that any *habitant* wishing to leave the city would

5-8 Montage of Britain's 1759 victories, including those of Niagara and Québec. The kingdom of George II had triumphed in North America, the Caribbean, Europe, India, and on the oceans.

5-9 Medallion commemorating the capture of Québec in 1759. Obverse: bust of Britannia beneath a laurel wreath over a crossed trident and standard and the names of Saunders and Wolfe. Reverse: Victory holds aloft a palm branch and a laurel wreath. Before her stands a trophy of arms at the foot of which is seated a bound captive.

5-10

have to acquire and show a passport. His intention was to prevent food and ammunition being secretly taken to the French Army. He then sent a letter to all the parishes of the Québec Government ordering the militiamen to turn in their weapons to their captain for safekeeping. A few days later he followed up with a manifesto in French, in which he urged the *habitants* to stay calm since they shouldn't expect anything from "an army that was weak, defeated, and, overcome, and was without resources." Lastly, in mid-November, Murray introduced a series of new rules aimed at restricting passage into and out of the walled city, with punishment to be meted out to any violators.

In addition to having their freedoms restricted, the civilian population was forced to endure very difficult living conditions. In the city, the British seized those homes that were still inhabitable. Nearly all the bourgeois families, finding their homes confiscated or being forced to share their lodgings with large numbers of soldiers, opted to abandon the city. Furthermore, as the bishop of Québec, Monseigneur de Pontbriand, noted, "the people of the city lack wood for the winter... [They are] without bread, without flour, without meat, and living only on the bits of biscuit and pork that English soldiers sell from their rations. Such is the situation to which the wealthiest townspeople are reduced; you can imagine the misery of the ordinary people and the poor."

Provide Assistance or They Will Perish

The French Army, meanwhile, was struggling with a much different set of concerns. While the Chevalier de Lévis held his position in the Jacques-Cartier River sector, Vaudreuil was worried. Having retreated to Montreal together with Intendant Bigot, he feared that Commander Amherst would try to attack Montreal from Lake Champlain, as the "capture of Québec would surely spur him to do the same." The French troops were therefore on high alert. However, Amherst, well aware that the majority of the French Army was assembled and expecting him to attack, decided to hold off the offensive until the following year. With the 1759

campaign finally over, Vaudreuil was able to call his troops back to their winter quarters. His land troops were housed among the inhabitants of various Montreal Government parishes, while the militia were urged to return home.

Getting the troops into their winter quarters was a priority, as the army simply no longer had the means to feed its men. Consequently, Vaudreuil left only 500 soldiers at Fort Jacques-Cartier. Intendant Bigot was only too aware of the problem, and spent all his time trying to get his hands on food supplies. He ordered the soldiers to seize all the oxen, cows, sheep, and wheat they could find in the surroundings. The French Army's purveyor general, Joseph Cadet, assisted Bigot in this task. Since the Royal Navy had left the St. Lawrence, he sent a request to some French merchants to obtain the supplies needed for the upcoming campaign and even made his own ships available to have the supplies transported to the colony.

In Montreal, Lévis and Vaudreuil teamed up with Bigot and Cadet to submit multiple requests to the French authorities. On November 7, the governor petitioned the Secretary of State of the Marine, Nicolas-René Berryer, for supplies: "We are even more threatened by a famine whose consequences would certainly be fatal, regardless of the fate of this colony [...] The very conservation of Canada in the hands of the King depends on this relief. I shall not deny, Monseigneur, that, despite all the efforts and industry of the purveyor, the misery shall be so great this winter that His Majesty may lose many of his subjects."

Mindful of the upcoming campaign, the Chevalier de Lévis wrote to the Secretary of State for War, the Duc de Belle-Isle, requesting reinforcements:

If the King wishes to sustain this colony, [he must] send, come the month of May, a squadron that shall precede that of England and render us masters of the river, with six thousand landing troops and four thousand recruits for the battalions and troops of the Marine stationed here. [...] We shall also need a train of heavy artillery with munitions of every calibre, such as iron, steel, tools of every kind, and ten thousand muskets [...]. If the King should deem it unnecessary to come to our aid, I must advise you not to count on us at the end of the month of May. We shall be obliged to surrender from sheer misery. Deprived of all necessities, we shall be left with nothing but courage, and no resources to put it to use.

On November 10, Lévis urged the Duc de Choiseul, Secretary of State for Foreign Affairs, to make peace before springtime, but the latter was already actively drawing up a bold strategy—the invasion of Great Britain. By directly attacking the British Isles, France hoped to sow panic among the enemy, create doubt in financial and political circles, and thereby put itself in a position of strength to quickly negotiate an advantageous peace agreement. However, the plan was aborted. On November 20, a large contingent from the French fleet, consisting of 21 warships, was taken by surprise and defeated by the Royal Navy in Quiberon Bay, just off the coast of Brittany. Following this humiliating defeat, the French Marine was no longer in any position to dispute the British Navy's mastery of the seas, much less come to the aid of its own colonies.

Lévis remained determined to obtain reinforcements. François-Marc-Antoine Le Mercier, Commander of the Artillery, was tasked with explaining

"If the King should deem it unnecessary to come to our aid, I must advise you not to count on us at the end of the month of May."

François-Gaston de Lévis

5-11

5-11 Also known as the "Bataille des Cardinaux," the Battle of Quiberon Bay took place on November 20, 1759, off the coast of Brittany. By the end of the attack, France had suffered 2,500 casualties and the loss of six ships, while Great Britain reported 300 dead and two ships sunk.

5-12

"The fatigues of the winter was so great that the living almost envied the dead."

British soldier

5-12 This view of Montreal is one of a series of 28 illustrations depicting various North American landscapes published in London in 1768 under the title *Scenographia Americana*.

to the king the colony's needs in terms of men and equipment. For Lévis, time was of the essence, as he was only too aware that, come summer, he would be under attack from three directions: Québec, Lake Ontario, and Lake Champlain.

Overwintering

In Québec, the winter of 1760 was a difficult time for the 7,000 men who made up the British garrison. The weather in December was bitterly cold, and finding firewood was a challenge. The soldiers would have to travel long distances, braving the cold and, in many cases, losing their fingers or toes to frostbite in the process. The sentinels, too, were exposed to the harsh winter conditions during their long watches, and some of them even succumbed to the cold.

In addition to their isolation and the unusually cold winter, the garrison also suffered considerably from the lack of fresh food, leading to an epidemic of scurvy that struck down part of the troops. As one soldier wrote: "A severe winter, now commenced, while we were totally unprepared for a such climate, [with] neither fuel, forage, or indeed anything, to make life tolerable. The troops were crowded inside vacant houses, as well as possible, numbers fell sick, and the scurvy made a dreadful havoc among us. [...] The fatigues of the winter was so great that the living almost envied the dead." By the end of the season, 2,312 members of the garrison had been hospitalized, and 682 had perished.

The Chevalier de Lévis spent the winter planning how to recapture Québec, the only point of access for the reinforcements that had been requested from Versailles. He was keenly aware that he would have to act quickly and lead the campaign before the snow was completely melted and the St. Lawrence became free of ice. He would also have to march on Québec before the British troops stationed at Lake Ontario and Lake Champlain converged on Montreal, in what he was convinced was the *"grand et essentiel objectif"* of the 1760 campaign for the British. Once the capital was retaken, Lévis would dispatch the French Army to Lake Champlain or the Upper St. Lawrence, where the threat was greatest. But first

and foremost, Lévis planned to take up position on the Plains of Abraham so as to be ready to bombard the city as soon as the artillery and reinforcements arrived from France. In preparation for his plan, he stepped up his efforts, not without some difficulty, to gather the material and food supplies his troops would need.

With regard to troops, Lévis would be able to count on virtually every last soldier in the colony, as well as on the militia, even those of the Québec Government. Despite pledging allegiance to King George II, the men remained loyal to France. After the capitulation of Québec, the local population did everything it could to reduce its collaboration with the British to the bare minimum and to avoid any direct confrontation that might provoke retaliation. It was a deft display of cautious resistance on the part of the people. While complying with the orders of the conquerors, they still managed to pass on information to the French Army and support the troops on a number of expeditions aimed at keeping the British garrison on high alert and gradually wearing it down.

To put his plan into action, Lévis assembled eight battalions of regular soldiers—where Montcalm had had only five—and virtually every available militiaman, leaving only one small detachment under the orders of Bougainville to defend Île aux Noix, on the Richelieu River, and another that he entrusted to Pierre Pouchot, who was in command of Fort Lévis in the Upper St. Lawrence. On March 29, with the melting ice on the verge of making the St. Lawrence River once again navigable, the Chevalier de Lévis wrote to his battalion commanders ordering them to stand ready: "We are approaching the moment at which the army shall assemble and march." □

Chapter Six

RETALIATION

Preparations

By early April 1760, the Chevalier de Lévis was impatient to set sail for Québec. As he waited, he refined his attack plan and saw to the final preparations. The Marquis de Vaudreuil offered his support, and began mobilizing his troops. On April 16, Vaudreuil dispatched a flurry of letters and orders. Since the Trois-Rivières and Montreal militia had already joined up with the army, he wrote to the captains of the Québec Government militia to ensure they would take up arms and join the army in great numbers: "You are only too familiar with the British aversion for all *Canadiens*. [...] As such, you can surely imagine your fate should they gain entire possession of this colony. [...] You are on the verge of triumphing against this enemy, who shall be forced to succumb to the efforts of our army. We are also poised to receive substantial relief from France. It is up to you, brave *Canadiens*, to distinguish yourselves; you must do everything you can, you must risk everything to protect your religion and for the well-being of your homeland."

To ensure the militiamen answered the call with enthusiasm and vigour, Vaudreuil ordered the priests of the Québec Government to wield the influence they held over their parishioners to convince them they should "all join the army for the sake of their religion, their honour, and their own interests." A manifesto was sent to the deserters who had joined the ranks of the British Army,

6-1

6-1 François-Gaston de Lévis took over as commander of France's regular troops on the death of the Marquis de Montcalm. The forty-year-old had considerable experience on the battlefields of Europe and had earned an excellent reputation.

urging them to rejoin their countrymen in exchange for amnesty. Meanwhile, Vaudreuil posted lookouts at strategic points on the St. Lawrence Estuary who were tasked with spotting any French ships sent to provide assistance to the troops and to provide them with captains experienced at navigating the waters of the St. Lawrence all the way to Québec.

On April 18, Lévis gave the order to all the battalions to be ready to march in two days' time. The men immediately began loading the smaller boats and preparing the frigates *Atalante* and *Pomone* that would escort and supply the troops. The Fort Jacques-Cartier garrison was on high alert, ready to join the army when it marched through. When he left Montreal on April 20, Lévis knew that to take back Québec, he would have at his disposal nearly 4,000 regular soldiers divided into five brigades of two battalions, 3,000 militiamen, and approximately 400 Indigenous warriors. Vaudreuil, meanwhile, remained in Montreal, ready to reinforce the borders of Lake Champlain and Lake Ontario as needed.

James Murray, who was entrenched in Québec, knew that the enemy would soon be back. On April 21, a proclamation he had posted in the city's public places caused a huge commotion: With the French Army preparing to besiege the city, the *habitants* had three days to pack up their personal belongings and leave the city, and they should not consider returning until they had permission to do so. Meanwhile, Murray ordered his troops to be ready to make camp.

His objective was to take up position in Sainte-Foy to be ready to support his three advance posts that were entrenched, respectively, on the heights of Cap-Rouge, at the Sainte-Foy Church, and at the Ancienne-Lorette Church, and to head off any landing attempt by the French. However, given the frigid temperature and the weakened state of his soldiers, Murray decided to forego this manoeuvre. His defence plan also called for entrenchments to be dug on the Plains of Abraham, but his men ran into difficulties there, too, with Murray noting in his journal: "This day, augmented the working party [...] with one hundred men, though that work advanced but slowly, the ground being so hard they could not drive their piquets above nine inches into it."

6-2

6-2 James Murray, governor of the Québec garrison since October 12, 1759, had the difficult task of maintaining discipline within his troops who were cut off from the world and had been decimated by disease while preparing the city for an attack by the French Army.

6-3 This map of the surroundings of Québec shows the positions of the French and British armies in April 1760, notably in Cap-Rouge, Ancienne-Lorette (known then simply as Lorette), Sainte-Foy, and Sillery.

The Return

Meanwhile, the French fleet was slowly easing its way through the ice: On April 22, the regiments camped near Trois-Rivières; then in Sainte-Anne, Grondines, and Deschambault the following night; and on April 24, they were in Pointe-aux-Trembles–Neuville–some twenty kilometres (12 miles) from Cap-Rouge. Lévis had three field cannons unloaded and sent scouts to confirm the enemy positions. His plan was to descend the river to Saint-Augustin, find shelter for his fleet, and cross the Cap-Rouge River on foot and on horseback at Ancienne-Lorette before heading to the heights of Sainte-Foy. Up until that point, he was sure the British were unaware he and his troops were on the march. That same day, Vaudreuil, who had received a message, informed Lévis that Gaspé Bay had already been free of ice for over three weeks. In order to allow the reinforcements from France to set sail up the river, the men there had "toiled with such zeal that, not only did

they break the ice, they also sawed into pieces those blocks that were too thick."

On April 26, Lévis and his troops finally reached Saint-Augustin. The boats were dragged over the ice to the shore, and the men set out on foot with three pieces of artillery, ammunition, and enough food for three days. Bourlamaque headed up the advance guard made up of grenadiers, volunteers, and Indigenous warriors in the direction of Ancienne-Lorette. When they got to the Cap-Rouge River, the first troops set about laying down bridges to allow the army behind them to cross without too much difficulty. A British detachment observed the French advance and decided to retreat back to Sainte-Foy. Once they had secured and crossed the Cap-Rouge River, Bourlamaque and his men continued their march. By nightfall, they had crossed a marsh and taken up position in a wooded area at the foot of the Sainte-Foy promontory.

Behind them, Lévis and his men struggled to cross the Cap-Rouge River. One of his officers, a man by

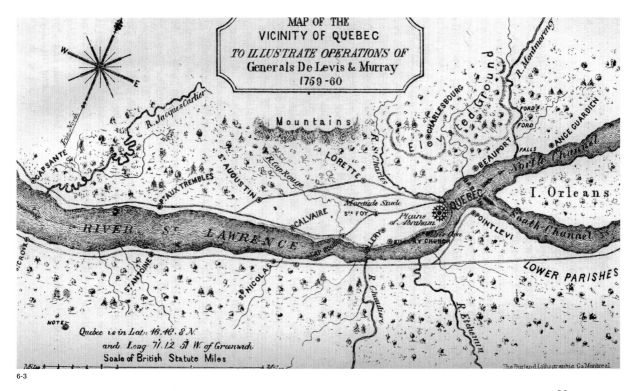

the name of La Pause, reported that "there was a most terrible storm; the ground was still covered with snow; it was bitterly cold, and we could see only by the glimmer of lightning. It took the troops the entire night to finally make their way across the river, the floodwaters having virtually washed away the bridges, and by daybreak they were in a most miserable state, shivering from the cold, without fire, and soaked to the skin." The army troops collapsed in exhaustion, resting for a few hours in some barns in Ancienne-Lorette.

On Watch

Early on the morning of April 27, Lévis finally caught up with Bourlamaque's advance guard. As he waited for his cannons to arrive, he observed the church and *habitations* of Sainte-Foy, where Murray had gathered some 3,000 men after learning of the enemy troops' approach. In fact, during the night of April 26, a French *canonnier*, whose boat sunk after being crushed by an ice floe, had managed to clamber out of the sinking craft and onto a chunk of ice that drifted all the way to Québec. Upon hearing his cries for help, some British sailors hauled him out of the water. He soon confessed that the French Army was approaching, escorted by seven ships with artillery and supplies aboard. At the news, Murray hurriedly assembled his troops and set out for Sainte-Foy.

The Chevalier de Lévis assembled his troops at the foot of the Sainte-Foy promontory. His plan was to launch an assault on the escarpment, but conditions were far from ideal: rain was falling steadily, the troops were tired, the artillery had yet to arrive, and the weapons were in poor shape. All these factors, combined with the difficult terrain and the fact the British were already present and in large numbers, and were keeping up heavy cannon and gun fire, prompted Lévis to delay the attack. Instead, he decided to wait until nightfall before attempting to scale the escarpment.

Murray, who was watching the enemy numbers grow, was informed that two French ships appeared to be preparing to land. Fearing his troops would be surrounded, he decided to order his men back inside the city walls, but not before blowing up

"There was a most terrible storm; the ground was still covered with snow; it was bitterly cold, and we could see only by the glimmer of lightning."

Jean-Guillaume de La Pause

the Sainte-Foy Church, which housed supplies and ammunition. Bourlamaque and his men kept up the pressure on the British rear guard, forcing the enemy to withdraw hastily to the safety of the city.

The pursuit had been exhausting for both sides. As Aide-Major Maurès de Malartic reported, "All did suffer […] from the rain, the snow, and the struggle of walking in water up to their knees." Aware of the state of exhaustion of his troops, Lévis decided to hole up in the houses around the Sainte-Foy Church and in the woods in Sillery rather than continuing on to the heights of Québec. In the city, the British garrison, too, was wearied and indisposed by the nonstop rain. The men received a double ration of rum and set about removing the boards from the ruined homes in the city to build fires to warm themselves and dry their clothing. Murray ordered his men posted at Point Lévis to burn down their blockhouse, sabotage their weapons, and destroy the provisions, then join him on the other side of the river at the next tide. The battle was imminent.

The Battle

On the morning of April 28, 1760, James Murray sized up the situation:

Prisoners, Deserters, and Spies

In the 18th century, military intelligence was gathered by every army and in every theatre of operations. In theory, the information gleaned provided an additional degree of security. In North America, during the Seven Years' War, the French and British armies alike employed the usual techniques for collecting secret information. They would interrogate prisoners and deserters, or turncoats, as they were also known. Deserters, especially, were eyed with suspicion. Perhaps they were spies? Nevertheless, while often uncertain in nature, military intelligence had its uses. ■

As I considered the enemy, so near at hand, would never suffer us to fortify the heights of Abraham; that even unmolested the chief engineer was of opinion it would take up ten days to execute the plan proposed; that the garrison was so sickly it could hardly be supposed equal to the task of guarding both town and lines; having also a strong confidence in troops who had hitherto been successful, I resolved to give the enemy battle before they could establish themselves.

Consequently, at seven o'clock in the morning, he gave the order to go into battle, and at nine o'clock, he headed out of the city gates.

At the head of an army of 3,800 men, Murray took up position in virtually the same spot on the Plains of Abraham that James Wolfe had occupied a few months earlier, only this time the pastures were covered in snow patches and puddles of water. He opted for a battle formation in two lines, in order to take up as much space as possible, and aligned eighteen six- and twelve-pounder cannons and two mortars. With the help of a large number of cannons positioned between his battalions, Murray knew he could inflict heavy losses on Lévis if the French commander was foolhardy enough to launch an attack.

According to Ensign Malcom Fraser, an officer with the 78th Highlanders Regiment, "[Murray] having a rising ground, whereon he might form his Army and plant his Cannon, so as to play on the Enemy as they advanced for about four hundred or five hundred yards with round shot, and when they came within a proper distance the grape shot must have cut them to pieces."

Meanwhile, the Chevalier de Lévis was convinced that Murray was busy ensuring the city's defences and that he was unlikely to engage in battle, so he focused on setting up camp and distributing supplies to his army, and set out to reconnoitre a site for a depot at Anse au Foulon and to determine the positions his troops would take up. The French Army emerged from the Sillery forest along Chemin Sainte-Foy, backed by three pieces of light artillery. Unlike Montcalm, Lévis did not incorporate the militiamen into his regular battalions. Instead, he opted to position them in platoons posted in front of or as support for the regular troops.

Spotting several enemy detachments outside the city walls, Lévis took possession of an abandoned redoubt to observe them more closely. That is when he saw the British Army appear on the heights. He

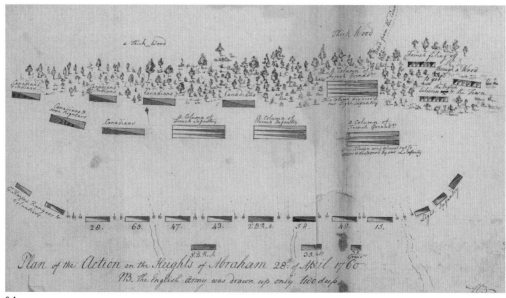

6-4

6-5

immediately ordered six battalions to take up position on the right, on either side of Chemin Saint-Louis, and commanded Bourlamaque and the La Sarre and Béarn battalions to head to the left, near the Dumont Mill and its outbuildings, along Chemin Sainte-Foy.

Murray was anxious to attack the enemy before they could form their battle line, so he abandoned his favourable position and ordered his men to advance. To begin with, his strategy worked. Pounded by cannon fire and strafed by grapeshot, the French troops suffered heavy casualties and were ordered to retreat to the edge of the Sillery forest. In fact, Lévis's plan was to reform his ranks there and structure his attack. On the left, Bourlamaque obeyed the order to retreat, although he deemed the manoeuvre risky, since the forest was swampy. While he was evacuating the Dumont Mill, Bourlamaque was wounded in the leg by cannon fire and his horse was killed. Overcoming this setback and despite the orders they had received, the troops making up the left launched a bayonet charge against the enemy, who was in an increasingly disadvantageous position.

As John Knox reported, conditions on the ground were not conducive to a British charge: "In the course of the action we were insensibly drawn from our advantageous situation into low swampy ground, where our troops fought almost knee-deep in dissolving wreaths of snow and water, whence it was utterly impracticable to draw off our artillery under those unhappy circumstances, after this

6-5 The parish priest of Québec, Father Jean-Félix Récher, who witnessed the events of 1759 and 1760, noted his observations about the battle of April 28, 1760, in his journal: "[It was] a most lively and sustained battle."

6-6 This tanbark mill owned by trader Jean-Baptiste Dumont found itself at the heart of the Battle of Sainte-Foy, on April 28, 1760. The mill was heavily damaged in the battle, and was destroyed several years later. In 2011, an archeological dig unearthed vestiges of the mill.

6-4 This map showing the positions of the French and British armies prior to the battle on April 28, 1760, appears in the journal attributed to Lieutenant Colonel Henry Fletcher of the British Army's 35th infantry regiment.

6-6

6-7

enfeebled army had performed prodigies of valour exceeding all description." Furthermore, his marching troops were impeding his cannon fire, depriving Murray of a considerable advantage.

The bayonet attacks launched by the La Sarre and Béarn battalions forced the British troops back beyond the Dumont Mill. When Lévis witnessed the success of the attacks of his left brigade, he ordered the right, waiting in the forest, to charge. Most of the Indigenous warriors, who were not used to fighting on open ground, opted to remain in the woods. Nevertheless, the manoeuvre worked, and the attack caused the British left flank to falter and the line to fall apart. To avoid his troops being completely surrounded, Murray abandoned the dead and wounded, and the bogged-down artillery, and ordered his men to retreat within the city walls. As Intendant Bigot reported, the French troops who followed in hot pursuit, bayonets in hand, were so exhausted that "they barely touched them, without finding the strength to run them through."

The battle lasted three hours, and the outcome was deadly, with considerable losses on both sides: Lévis reported 193 dead and 640 wounded, while Murray assessed his casualties at 292 dead, 837 wounded, and 53 prisoners. Most of the wounded, French and British alike, were treated at the Hôpital général. As one nun noted: "For the twenty-hours during which the wounded were transported, we were forced to endure the cries of the dying and the agony of the wounded [...] After making up more than five hundred beds we were provided from the King's storehouses, there were still just as many who needed them. Our barns and stables were filled with these unfortunate souls. [...] Everywhere we looked were maimed arms and legs."

A Waiting Game

While this French victory caused very little reaction in Versailles, it rattled the convictions of the British parliamentarians, including Horace Walpole, who exclaimed: "Who the deuce was thinking of Quebec? America was like a book one has read and done with, [...] but here we are on a sudden reading our book

Hôpital général

As soon as the British Army began to shell Québec in July 1759, the Augustine order of Hôtel-Dieu, the Ursuline nuns, and many of the city's *habitants* sought refuge at the Hôpital général, located in the Lower Town near the St. Charles River, out of range of the cannon fire. The night after the Battle of the Plains of Abraham, the British seized possession of the building and converted it into a military hospital. The injured on both sides were cared for there, and the dead were buried in the adjacent cemetery. In the wake of his victory on April 28, 1760, the Chevalier de Lévis retook the Hôpital général. Considered a neutral zone, the hospital became a safe place for dialogue and negotiations between the two warring sides. When the hospital reverted back under British control in May, it gradually regained its original vocation as a hospice. ■

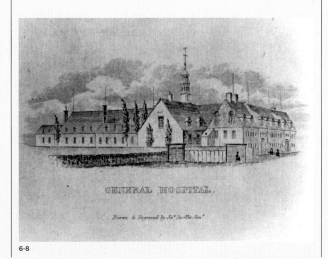

GENERAL HOSPITAL.

6-8

backwards." The situation was also worrisome for William Pitt, who was increasingly isolated in London in his conviction that the hostilities should be kept up until France was completely defeated. If the city of Québec was retaken by the French Army, it would be impossible to organize a second major offensive to seize it again, as there was a strong wave of pacificism overtaking the country, and if a treaty were to be signed in such circumstances, Canada would surely remain in the bosom of France.

In Québec, it wasn't a time for diplomacy but, rather, a time for action as the French Army prepared to besiege the city. At Anse au Foulon, there was a steady back-and-forth traffic of boats: food supplies were stored there, and the artillery needed for the siege was hoisted up to the Plains of Abraham. The troops took up their positions barely 600 metres (about 2,000 feet) from the fortifications, and dug trenches from the Buttes à Neveu all the way to the Saint-Louis Gate. They also got to work erecting batteries. Although he had only a limited number of pieces of artillery, Lévis had every intention of breaching the fortified walls.

"America was like a book one has read and done with, […] but here we are on a sudden reading our book backwards."

Horace Walpole

6-9

While morale was high in the French camp, the same couldn't be said for the British troops, who had struggled to keep their spirits up since their defeat on April 28. Panic-stricken and desperate, the soldiers stripped the storehouses and city homes of alcohol, and proceeded to drink themselves into a stupor. The men were fearful of what awaited them as besieged soldiers in hostile territory. On April 30, in an attempt to rein in the soldiers' misbehaviour and re-establish discipline in the ranks, Murray had one of the delinquent soldiers hanged, to set an example. The next day, John Knox noted an immediate shift in attitude among the men: "We are roused from a lethargy; we have recovered our good humour, our sentiments for glory, and we seem, one and all, determined to defend our dearly purchased garrison to the last extremity."

With his army now more inclined to fight, Murray continued his manoeuvres aimed at delaying as long as possible the enemy's progress on its entrenchments and batteries. He had embrasures made in the city's curtain walls and ramparts, and positioned new artillery there that proceeded to fire nonstop on the French men carrying out the work. Even though he had sent a request for reinforcements to Louisbourg and Halifax, Murray knew he had to proceed with caution and alter his strategy. With his reserves of munitions stocks quickly dwindling, he soon had no choice but to order his artillerymen to cut back on their firing frequency against Lévis and his men.

On May 9, before the French batteries were even operational, word of a ship spotted sailing upriver spread like wildfire. The tension was palpable in both camps. However, the French troops' hopes were dashed when they saw the ship respond to the salute from within the city walls. When it passed in front of Point Lévis, the men immediately recognized the *Lowestoft* flying its British flag. Murray's army was jubilant, as Knox attested in his journal: "About eleven o'clock, [...] we had the inconceivable satisfaction to behold the *Leostoffe* frigate sail up into the bason and come to an anchor [...] The gladness of the troops is not to be expressed: both Officers and soldiers mounted the parapets in the face of the enemy, and huzzaed, with their hats in the air, for almost an hour."

The Outcome

Vaudreuil, who was still in Montreal, was shaken by the news, and he wrote to Lévis: "The arrival of an English frigate does not bode well for us." However, Lévis clung to the hope that he would soon receive the much-awaited reinforcements and that he and his men would be able to save the colony. On May 11, the French batteries finally opened fire, but the few pieces of artillery they had were in poor shape, and the powder was stale and ineffective. Since the French Army's reserves of powder were as low as that of the British, each piece of artillery was limited to twenty strikes per twenty-four-hour period.

Lévis grew increasingly dismayed at his troops' inability to breach the city walls. In a letter to Vaudreuil, he wrote: "You can surely imagine my despair at all the accidents and misfortunes that have befallen us; if only we had had a little luck on our side, we would certainly have succeeded, but, alas, we must acquiesce to the whims of Providence." In the same breath, he urged the governor general to immediately do everything in his power to amass food supplies in the Government of Montreal, as they would be essential to defend the heart of the colony in the event the siege of Québec were to fail.

During the night of May 15, the Royal Navy's *Vanguard* and the *Diana* also reached Québec. Lévis was forced to accept the facts: "I fear that France has abandoned us, as the winds have been blowing from the northeast for many a day, and the tides have been high, and yet nothing has arrived. We have done, and continue to do, all we can. I believe the colony is lost without resources, if no relief is to arrive."

But no relief ever did arrive. The British Navy's crushing victory in the Battle of Quiberon Bay had dealt a serious blow to the French Marine, making it unlikely the colony could be saved. Versailles did manage to dispatch a small squadron carrying provisions, ammunition, and 400 soldiers, but no heavy artillery. The relief convoy left Bordeaux on April 10 and, despite being partly intercepted by the British, managed to make it to the Gulf of St. Lawrence on May 14, however on learning they had been beaten to the punch by the British, they sought refuge at the mouth of the Ristigouche River, in the Bay of Chaleurs. They were blockaded there by the

FREGATE DE 40. CANONS

On a marqué à l'article précédent, le défaut des petits Bâtiments qui ont une batterie basse, c'est pourquoi, on represente la fregate de 40. canons A, n'ayant qu'une Batterie, et des Gaillards. On construit d'autres Fregattes entre celle cy et la Corvette B, leurs proportions sont marquées à la 22.e Planche.

Les Fregates, et corvetes, sont les decouvertes des armées; elles se tiennent dans les Combats, a portée de secourir les Vaisseaux désemparés, et d'empecher autant qu'elles peuvent, les Brulots Ennemis d'en aprocher. Il y en a que l'on destine, pour repeter les signaux, et porter les ordres du general aux differents endroits de l'armée: on les employe dans d'autres occurrences, à convoyer des flottes marchandes, et aux Commissions où les grands Bâtiments ne sont point necessaires.

6-10

6-10 On May 16, 1760, the French and British ships that faced off on the St. Lawrence River had one thing in common: the *Atalante*, the *Pomone*, the *Lowestoft*, and the *Diana* were all frigates. They were of intermediate size, meaning they were swift and manoeuvrable, and their cannons were all mounted on the same gun deck.

British, and, eventually, the men abandoned and scuttled the ships that July.

With the arrival of the new British ships, Lévis ordered his boats at Anse au Foulon to withdraw and sail back up the river to safety. But it was too late. While the *Vanguard* bombarded the French Army's entrenchments and infrastructure, the *Lowestoft* and the *Diana* gave chase to the ships that had been supporting the siege. In its attempt to avoid capture, the frigate *Pomone* ran aground at Anse au Foulon, as did some of the smaller boats at the mouth of the Cap-Rouge River. As for the *Atalante*, she continued to fight at Pointe-aux-Trembles, where, after running out of gunpowder, she was sunk.

On land, the French Army spent the day of May 16 withdrawing their artillery, gathering all the provisions the men could carry, and destroying the rest. Lévis and his troops began marching during the night and reached the Cap-Rouge River at daybreak. They spent the next two days unloading their stranded vessels of all the supplies and ammunition they could salvage, then continued marching towards the Jacques-Cartier River, which they crossed on May 20. The Siege of Québec was thus officially lifted, and the French retreat to Montreal had begun.

Lévis did, however, leave behind a unit of about 1,800 men under the orders of Jean-Daniel Dumas, the same commander who had taken by surprise and defeated Edward Braddock at the Monongahela River in 1755. The French troops were dispatched to three locations: Pointe-aux-Trembles, Fort Jacques-Cartier, and Deschambault. Their mission was to observe the British movements both on land and on the river. The rest of the French soldiers headed to Montreal, where they returned to their winter quarters in the homes of the *habitants*, as the authorities simply didn't have the resources to feed them. The officers and soldiers, alike, however, were instructed to be ready to march as ordered. As for the members of the militia, while some of them followed the army, most returned to their homes, as did the Indigenous warriors. Morale among the French ranks was at an all-time low, and there was a pervading feeling that they had been abandoned. When Bougainville, who was posted at Île aux Noix, on the Richelieu River, was informed of what had transpired in Québec, he couldn't believe it: "I cannot conceive that not even a single corvette was dispatched to warn us that we couldn't—or wouldn't—be relieved. Never have troops found themselves in such a position as ourselves."

James Murray's troops were boosted by the prospect of an imminent and conclusive victory. Merchant vessels loaded with supplies arrived in Québec to provision the garrison. Following Saunders' instructions to the letter, Alexander Colvill left Halifax and also sailed to the city. As he sailed up the St. Lawrence, he made a point of stationing warships at strategic points along the way, guaranteeing his army full control of the waterway. The British vise was inexorably tightening around the French Army that had been pushed back to and surrounded in the very heart of the colony. ☐

Chapter Seven

EN ROUTE TO PEACE

A Three-pronged Strategy

Although the French Army now controlled only the centre of Canada, the Secretary of State of Foreign Affairs, the Duc de Choiseul, remained seemingly optimistic, writing in a letter to Voltaire: "The English shall not keep Canada. I beg you not to judge the play before having seen the conclusion. Perhaps we are merely at Act III. While the catastrophe was unfortunate, I am preparing for you a fifth act in which virtue shall be rewarded."

Yet, in the North American theatre of war, the Chevalier de Lévis, with his 2,000 men, was no match for the powerful British war machine commanded by Jeffery Amherst. Having taken possession of Québec and the enemy positions on Lake Champlain and Lake Ontario, the British Army kept up its three-pronged strategy. It was a strategy developed during the 1759 campaign which consisted of attacking the French Army simultaneously on three fronts with a view to surrounding and wiping it out. With Lévis and his troops retreating to Montreal, a contingent of more than 18,000 men was set to converge on that city. Backed by an impressive fleet of ships, James Murray sailed up the St. Lawrence from Québec with 3,800 men, while Brigadier William Haviland and his 3,400 men arrived from Crown Point, south of Lake Champlain, via the Richelieu River. Meanwhile, Jeffery Amherst, set out from Oswego

7-1

7-1 Étienne François, the Duc de Choiseul, was appointed Secretary of State of Foreign Affairs on December 3, 1758.

and descended the St. Lawrence rapids from Lake Ontario with 11,000 men under his command.

But before it could engage in hostilities, the British Army needed time to coordinate its attack, position its troops, and gather supplies and ammunition. In Québec, Murray drafted a proclamation (in French) that he had circulated in the governments of Trois-Rivières and Montreal. His message was part threatening, part conciliatory, and aimed to quell any hint of rebellion by the *habitants* during his march against Montreal: "*Canadiens*! Retreat and lay down your arms; remain in your habitations, and provide no assistance to our enemies. Respect these conditions and your tranquility shall not be interrupted; our soldiers shall contain themselves and shall inflict no damage on your fields. You still have time to avoid famine and plague–both more devastating than war, and both at this very moment threatening Canada with total and irreparable ruin."

In Debt

On May 29, 1760, Lévis finally met up with the Marquis de Vaudreuil in Montreal and shared his thoughts on what steps they would need to take to be able to defend the colony again. The two men agreed on the importance of gathering food supplies and repairing their army's weaponry, and decided that reinforcements should be sent to Île aux Noix to help Bougainville slow Haviland's march, as well as to Fort Lévis to allow Commander Pouchot to delay Amherst's advance. They also agreed on the need to encourage the *habitants* and the Indigenous warriors to take up arms again. And lastly, they decided to have a number of boats and other small watercraft built to defend the rivers, including the Richelieu River.

Even more pressing was the need to restore discipline among the regular troops. In a bid to halt the wave of desertions since the end of the Siege of Québec, Lévis ordered his battalion commanders to take firm action: "You must do the right thing and seize all the soldiers in your regiment who have taken leave of the army without permission, and

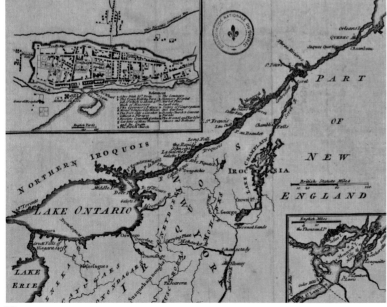

7-2

7-2 Map of the Amherst Expedition from Oswego, on Lake Ontario, to Montreal.

France's Debt

In the 17th century, to make up for a lack of cash, France paid the expenses it incurred in Canada in the name of the king in paper currency by means of one of four financial instruments: card money, certificates, treasury notes known as *ordonnances*, or bills of exchange. Bills of exchange were drawn on funds allocated to cover the expenses of the colony and were payable in cash in France once a year. By 1754, Versailles was struggling to honour the increasing number of bills of exchange that were arriving every year from Canada. The colony was ordered to reduce its costs, but in the midst of war, that was all but impossible, with France's expenses in Canada rising sharply from 11 million livres in 1756 to 30 million livres in 1759. On October 15 of that year, Louis XV suspended payment of France's bills of exchange and postponed repayment of its Canadian debt until peace was restored. From that point on, paper money began trading well below its face value, and after the capitulation of the colony in September 1760, it was virtually worthless. The Treaty of Paris, which was signed February 10, 1763, called for France to settle its debt. After endless calculations and a long delay, Versailles finally paid off only about 38 million livres of its total debt of 83 million, a serious blow for the 8,000 or so people who still held paper money. ∎

to throw them in irons, my intention being to have them beaten every last one of them and, if there are great numbers of them, to have them decimated."

On June 13, while the French Army was busy organizing its defences, the letters sent from Versailles and carried by the relief ships that left from Bordeaux and were held up at the Ristigouche River, finally arrived over land in Montreal, where they were delivered to Lévis. The letters contained disturbing news. The king had passed a decree declaring that he was suspending payment of bills of exchange and deferring repayment of his Canadian debt until peace was restored. As a result, anyone who had provided goods or services to the State and its agents would not be paid in the foreseeable future. The news was met with widespread consternation by merchants, soldiers, and *habitants* alike.

In direct and immediate retaliation, the *habitants* refused to sell their grain and livestock to the agents tasked with scouring the countryside in search of food supplies. On June 30, Intendant Bigot announced that he had managed to "gather, with much difficulty, enough for a unit of four thousand men to subsist for one month." Vaudreuil, Lévis, and Bigot had no choice but to personally guarantee the *habitants* that their crops and animals would indeed be paid for by the State. The colonial authorities were desperate to win back the trust of the people by whatever means they could, so they would continue to take part in the war effort.

"Who can carry on or support the war without ships, artillery, ammunitions, or provisions?"

John Knox

Versailles's decision also had an impact on the regular troops. In a letter to the Secretary of State for War, the Duc de Belle-Isle, Lévis wrote, "Many of the officers have been forced to trade or sell their garments to survive and to have *ordonnances* issued by their families, since bills of exchange and currency are of little credit […]. The troops, with the exception of the La Sarre and Royal-Roussillon, have been stripped naked. […] We are in no condition to conduct the campaign, as we are lacking food, weaponry, and everything else; in fact, it is surprising that we are even still alive."

From a tactical standpoint, Lévis was under no illusions. He had already ceded the St. Lawrence to Murray, since he no longer had any back-up there. And as he had very few resources to shore up his troops at Île aux Noix and Fort Lévis, he knew he wouldn't be able to halt the British march; at best he could attempt to slow its progress. His only remaining hope was that the three advancing armies would fail to reassemble and coordinate their attack. Only then would he have any chance of confronting and defeating them, one at a time.

Montreal

In Québec, James Murray prepared to sail up the St. Lawrence. Given the harsh winter they had endured and the gruelling events of the spring, he took pains to allow his troops the time to recover fully. He also needed to assemble enough materiel for the upcoming campaign. At the same time, he had a duty to ensure the governance of the city and to maintain order there. On June 27, Murray had his men load the prisoners and deserters onto ships headed for England and France. It wasn't until a few days later, on July 2, that he finally allowed the city's *habitants* to return to Québec, albeit only after having their belongings inspected.

On July 14, Murray left behind 1,700 soldiers at the garrison in Québec, and had the rest of his men board 33 transport ships headed for Montreal, escorted by two frigates, two sloops, nine floating batteries, and 22 flat-bottomed ships. When the fleet passed Fort Jacques-Cartier, the French garrison fired on it, but to no effect, as the river was

Prisoners of War and the Wounded

On February 6, 1759, France and Great Britain signed an agreement known as the *Cartel de l'Écluse*, in which they set out the treatment to be reserved for the sick, wounded, and prisoners of their respective land troops. By the autumn of that same year, the status and sustenance of the wounded in Québec was the subject of negotiations between French and British military leaders. For one, should the wounded French soldiers admitted to the Hôpital général on September 13 be considered prisoners of war? After much dialogue, the British point of view prevailed: the hospital was deemed an extension of the battlefield, and the injured were considered captives. On April 28, 1760, when the Chevalier de Lévis took back possession of the Hôpital général, the prisoners were once again deemed simply patients. When he retreated to Montreal in May, Lévis requested that James Murray provide sustenance to the wounded French soldiers, and in agreeing, Murray once again made them prisoners. ■

7-3

7-4

"Thus are we caught on all sides."

François-Gaston de Lévis

7-4 To reach Montreal, Lieutenant Colonel Jeffery Amherst and his troops had to negotiate the St. Lawrence River Rapids, which were treacherous in some sections.

too wide at that point for the ships to be within range. Unable to inflict any damage on the enemy, Jean-Daniel Dumas decided to leave a detachment at Deschambault and follow the British fleet's progress from the north shore of the river.

As the British convoy advanced upriver, Murray dispatched land patrols to post manifestos (in French) on the doors of the churches along the way, ordering the *habitants* to surrender their weapons, failing which "the ravaging of their lands and the burning of their homes would be the least of their misfortunes." The goal in so doing was to incite the population to swear allegiance to King George II. John Knox summed up his commander's message in his journal: "Who can carry on or support the war without ships, artillery, ammunitions, or provisions? At whose mercy are your habitations, and that harvest which you expect to reap this summer, together with all you are possessed of in this world? Therefore consider your own interest and provoke us no more." On July 20, Murray himself attended a ceremony at which 55 men from Sainte-Croix and 79 others from Lotbinière swore their allegiance. Some of the *habitants* even consented to trade with the British troops, offering them butter, eggs, and milk in exchange for salt pork.

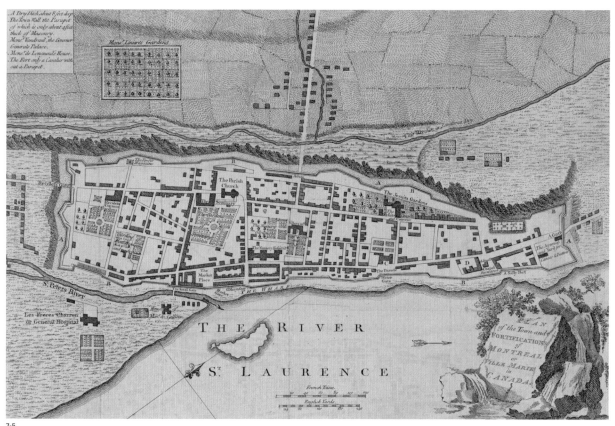

7-5

7-5 In 1760, the city of Montreal
was protected by a ditch some
two and a half metres (8 feet) deep
and by a masonry wall six metres
high (19½ feet) and two metres
(6½ feet) thick.

7-6

On August 12, Murray's fleet was joined by the battalions that had sailed from Louisbourg. At about the same time, the armies of Jeffery Amherst and William Haviland set sail, and on the 18th, the ships carrying Amherst and his men passed in front of Fort Lévis. Commander Pierre Pouchot had barely 300 men at his disposal to defend the fort. Two days later, the British began bombarding it, and the French troops responded as best they could, but, by August 25, with no more ammunition, his cannons no longer able to fire, and the fort in ruins, Pouchot was forced to surrender.

At Île aux Noix, the situation played out in much the same way. Tasked with defending the fort with only 1,300 regular soldiers, militiamen, and sailors, Bougainville was unable to withstand Haviland's siege for long. By August 27, after his fleet was captured, Bougainville's position had become untenable, and he resorted to quietly evacuating his men under the cover of night in the hopes they could join up with the French Army in Montreal. The Siege of Île aux Noix ended the next day when the fifty or so men who had remained behind gave themselves up to the British.

When he learned of these surrenders, Lévis wrote, "Thus are we caught on all sides." For Lévis,

the worst-case scenario was unfolding before him. The road to Montreal was now free, and the three armies met up as planned. Amherst was delighted, and noted in his journal: "I believe never three Armys, setting out from different and very distant Parts from each other joyned in the Center, as was intended, better than we did."

The End

On September 4, as the British approached, Lévis left the south shore of the St. Lawrence and reached the Island of Montreal. He also had his battalions retreat there, and posted them in different spots. With virtually no ammunition left, his 2,000 men could no longer continue to defend the city. The local population refused to take up arms, accusing the military authorities of seeking to use them as cannon fodder. At around eleven o'clock in the morning on September 6, Jeffery Amherst and his troops disembarked on the island and began marching towards the city. At eight o'clock in the evening, the Marquis de Vaudreuil called a council of war attended by the key officers of the land and Marine troops, as well as Intendant Bigot. He laid out the situation for them and proposed that the terms of surrender be drawn up. The men agreed it was in the colony's best interest to opt for a capitulation that would be advantageous for the population and honourable for the troops, instead of continuing to try to mount a defence that would merely delay their inevitable defeat by a few days.

The next day, Louis-Antoine de Bougainville and James Abercrombie, Amherst's aide-de-camp, were appointed as the emissaries of each army. Vaudreuil began by asking for a truce to be declared until October 1. His hope was that in the interim he would receive news from Europe announcing that the war was over and that peace had been restored. Amherst refused, instead offering a six-hour cease-fire. The negotiations continued. The British were in full control of the situation, and decided to impose a series of harsh terms of capitulation on the enemy: They intended to refuse to give the French ground and Marine troops the usual honours of war. The defeated army would have to lay down its arms and would not be allowed to serve any longer in the present conflict, whether in North America or in Europe. This was a serious affront to the French, and Bougainville attempted, in vain, to get Amherst to change his mind.

When he learned of the proposed articles of capitulation, Lévis was furious. Speaking on behalf of all his officers, he wrote a letter to Vaudreuil, noting, "This article of capitulation could not be more contrary to the service of the King and to the honour of his arms. [...] Consequently, we ask the Marquis M. de Vaudreuil to immediately call off all discussions with the English general and to take the most vigorous defensive action our current position allows us to. [...] It would be unheard-of for the troops to submit to such harsh and humiliating conditions without being under fire." Lévis urged Vaudreuil to cease the negotiations and grant him permission to launch a final battle for the honour of king and country.

Vaudreuil felt the interests of the colony must be protected, and he refused Lévis's demand, ordering him to comply with the terms of capitulation and lay down his arms. In a bid to avoid a measure of the humiliation to which his troops would be subjected, Lévis ordered his battalions to burn their regimental

"It would be unheard-of for the troops to submit to such harsh and humiliating conditions without being under fire."

François-Gaston de Lévis

7-6 The Capitulation of Montreal included 55 articles dealing with a range of topics, including the army; administration of the colony; religion; the return to France of soldiers and administrators; moveable and immoveable property; the Acadians; the Indigenous people; neutrality among citizens; civil law; and even the continued practice of slavery in Canada.

The Honours of War

In Europe, it was common practice for a besieging army to grant the honours of war to a defeated garrison in recognition of its valiant defence. The defeated troops would be allowed to march out of the town or fort with pipes and drums playing, colours flying, and weapons loaded, even sometimes with pieces of artillery, and to rejoin their army unimpeded. Conversely, refusing to grant the honours of war would be perceived as an attempt to humiliate the defeated party. In Jeffery Amherst's view, the atrocities committed by the French Army and its Indigenous allies, including during the capture of Fort William Henry in 1757, represented an unacceptable level of violence and fuelled a desire for revenge, culminating in the capitulation of Louisbourg in July 1758 and of Montreal in September 1760. Amherst therefore refused to grant the French Army the honours of war, despite its bravery. ■

7-7

flags rather than turn them over to the enemy. On September 8, the Capitulation of Montreal was signed. It was both harsher and more far-reaching than the one signed in Québec the previous year. The surrender did, however, offer an opening that somewhat lessened its severity. Article XIII stipulated that "If [...] news of Peace should arrive, and, that by treaty, Canada should remain to his most Christian Majesty, [...] every thing shall return to its former state [...], and the present capitulation shall become null and of no effect." In other words, Canada's fate would play out in Europe.

In the meantime, though, the French Army in North America would have to surrender. On September 9, a British detachment headed to Place d'Armes with its artillery. The defeated battalions filed past one by one, without their colours flying, to lay down their arms. Amherst was disturbed to see the soldiers without their regimental flags: "Had no Colours, and the commanding officers gave their word of Honour the Troops had none when they capitulated; that they had brought Colours here six years ago, found them troublesome in this Country, that they were quite torn and they had destroyed them. I made all the enquiry I could about this. It would be so scandalous for them to hide them after what they have said that I must believe them."

Once the battalions had surrendered their weapons, Lévis reviewed his troops. A British detachment then took possession of the city, and the sick and wounded were transported to Hôtel-Dieu Hospital. On September 10, 1760, to conclude the capitulation, Amherst dined with Vaudreuil (Lévis was conspicuously absent). The two commanders took the opportunity to discuss the situation in the colony, the assistance that never arrived from France, and Vaudreuil's impossible challenge of defending himself against three armies.

The news of the Capitulation of Montreal spread across Great Britain, including in the October issue of the *London Magazine*, which described the events in detail along with a map of the city. George II learned of his army's victory in North America only a short time before he passed away, on October 25, 1760. In France, Louis XV was furious to hear that Canada had been handed over to the British, and under anything but honourable conditions for his army.

The French Departure

The repatriation of the defeated troops to France, as set out in detail in the Articles of Capitulation, began on September 11, 1760. The British prepared the boats that would transport the men to Québec, where they would board ships bound for Europe. Before they left Montreal, Lévis reviewed his battalions one last time and conducted a headcount of 2,200 soldiers, including those in hospital. He gave instructions to the commanders of each of the battalions, ordering that their return to France be carried out in an orderly and disciplined fashion.

On September 14, the boarding of the ships bound for Québec began with the Languedoc and Berry regiments, as well as the Compagnies franches de la Marine. The next day saw the Royal-Roussillon, La Sarre, and Guyenne regiments embark, and on the 16th, the de La Reine and Béarn regiments set sail. Lévis's turn came on September 17, and Vaudreuil and Bigot left Montreal on September 20 and 21, respectively. In accordance with the Articles of Capitulation, Amherst ordered that the papers of the governor general, the intendant, and the supreme council of Québec, as well as the maps and charts necessary for the administration of the colony, be handed over to him.

The combination of violent winds and a shortage of food supplies made the journey to Québec particularly long and arduous. Lévis noted that "the battalions arrived there in tatters." Since it was already getting late in the season, the plan was for the troops to set sail for France as soon as possible. A total of 1,683 regular troop soldiers, 692 soldiers from the Compagnies franches de la Marine, and 507 sailors embarked aboard 22 ships, along with the civil servants, civilians, and clergymen who had chosen to leave the colony. The French soldiers who had found brides during the war chose to stay behind. As Lévis boarded a ship bound for France on October 18, he promised to impress on Versailles "the distinguished way in which [his troops] had served, and [to do everything] in his power to secure for them all the graces to which they are entitled." He set about doing exactly that as soon as he set foot in France on November 25.

7-8

7-8 In this work of propaganda, a benevolent Jeffery Amherst is depicted bringing bread to the people of Montreal, who bow and kneel before him in gratitude.

"So long as the said habitants shall obey and conform to the said orders, they shall enjoy the same privileges as the ancient subjects of the King, and they may rely on our protection."

Jeffery Amherst

The Military Regime

Since the war was not over and no treaty had yet been signed officially determining Canada's fate, the colony was governed by the occupying army. On September 22, 1760, before returning to his base in New York, Jeffery Amherst issued a proclamation. In an effort to maintain public order, he laid the groundwork for an interim government under the command of James Murray. The governments of Québec, Trois-Rivières, and Montreal were now districts, and Murray would head up the first, while the other two districts would fall under the authority of a military governor.

In a public placard posted in French and signed that same day, Amherst set out several rules for the population, including the obligation to hand over their weapons. In closing, he urged the people of Montreal to "receive and treat the troops as brothers and fellow citizens. It is further enjoined upon them to hearken to and obey all that is commanded them, whether by us or by their governors, and those having authority from us and them; and so long as the said habitants shall obey and conform to the said orders, they shall enjoy the same privileges as the ancient subjects of the King, and they may rely on our protection."

For the *Canadiens*, both in the cities and the countryside alike, their rights and obligations remained essentially the same as before the war, despite the oath of allegiance they were all forced to take. Concretely, they were allowed to continue ownership of their property, exercise their Catholic religion freely, and engage in trade. French civil law was also maintained. As a result, life slowly resumed, but the task was colossal. The *habitants* rebuilt their homes, outbuildings, churches, and rectories. They continued their day-to-day tasks of restoring their fields and farms to help relieve hunger. Those who had lost their spouses during the war or due to famine or disease remarried. Merchants and traders revived their business. Pupils went back to school. The Ursuline nuns in Québec took in their very first British boarders. Despite the relative calm, there was still a pervasive feeling of uncertainty. Payment of bills of exchange was still suspended, and in 1762, the district of Québec was once again faced with the prospect of famine. As people waited for peace to be restored, one question lingered: Would Canada remain under the yoke of His British Majesty or would it return to His Most Christian Majesty?

The Treaty of Paris

While the fighting in North America ended in September 1760, the war was still not over, and a certain weariness began to set in. George III, who had recently ascended to the throne, was against the idea of continuing the conflict, which he deemed bloody and costly. Early on in his reign, he distanced himself from his ministers, including William Pitt, who wanted to prolong an all-out war. The king wanted peace as soon as possible. In France, the Duc de Choiseul, appointed Secretary of State for War in January 1761 and of the Marine in October of the same year, was tapped by Louis XV to spearhead the peace talks. Choiseul's goal was to sign a peace agreement and immediately prepare France's revenge against Great Britain.

Madame de Pompadour, the king's chief mistress and favourite advisor, summed up this desire:

It is not a matter of achieving certain peace: such a thing is impossible, the English and French cannot remain friends for long; the reciprocal hatred of the two nations, the rivalry of trade, the opposition of interests and Alliances will soon have them taking up arms once again. This is why I believe we must strive to maintain several establishments in Africa and the Indies: it is the only way to repair and augment our Marine, salvage our trade, fortify our positions throughout, and attack the English with greater success and assurance when the occasion presents itself.

When the first round of negotiations got underway in 1761, France was not in a position of strength. It had no conquests it could use as bargaining chips for land handovers. It would have to do what it could to preserve its trade interests if it wanted to rebuild its army and regain its place in the diplomatic arena. Choiseul insisted that he was ready to cede Canada, and offered no resistance in

7-9

7-9 George III acceded to Great Britain's throne on October 25, 1760, and remained in power until 1820.

7-10 The Treaty of Paris bore the signatures of the respective negotiators for France, Great Britain, and Spain, namely César Gabriel Choiseul-Praslin; John Russell, 4th Duke of Bedford; and Jeronimo Grimaldi.

7-11 This allegorical engraving by Jean-Baptiste Tilliard entitled *Paix rendue à l'Europe* depicts the main countries involved in the conflict in the form of ancient goddesses.

that regard, however he was determined to retain control of the fisheries. Aside from the boards of trade of the seaboard, most of the interested parties in France supported him, as did its philosophers, including Voltaire, who was especially eloquent on the subject: "If I would so dare, I would implore you on bended knee to rid the Ministère de la France of Canada forever. If you lose it, you shall lose virtually nothing; if you wish it back, you shall receive only an eternal cause of war and humiliation."

The negotiations broke off when Spain joined the war alongside France in January 1762, but resumed again in the fall of the same year. Choiseul was determined to make gains in the colonies, and had his eye on the sugar islands in the Caribbean and their trade. Great Britain, meanwhile, had little interest in Canada and its resources. However, it knew full well that by obtaining the territory, it would consolidate its foothold in North America and assert its control over its older colonies.

A preliminary peace agreement was finally signed in Fontainebleau on November 3, 1762. In London,

Parliament ratified the agreement on December 9 with an overwhelming majority. Fighting officially ceased on the battlefields at the end of the year and, on February 10, 1763, the treaty was signed in Paris by France, Great Britain, and Spain. The document set out a list of which territories would be ceded, restored, or exchanged in the name of peace and, especially, in the name of trade.

In North America, Canada and Île Royale were ceded to Great Britain under Article 4:

His Most Christian Majesty renounces all pretensions which he has heretofore formed or might have formed to Nova Scotia or Acadia in all its parts, and guaranties the whole of it, and with all its dependencies, to the King of Great Britain: Moreover, his Most Christian Majesty cedes and guaranties to his said Britannick Majesty, in full right, Canada, with all its dependencies, as well as the island of Cape Breton, and all the other islands and coasts in the gulph and river of St. Lawrence, and in general, every thing that depends on the said countries, lands, islands, and coasts…

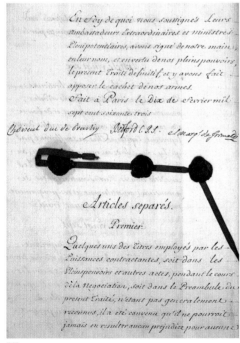

7-10

7-11

Louisiana was divided up between Great Britain and Spain. France lost everything in North America except for the islands of Saint-Pierre and Miquelon, and its fishing rights off the coast of Newfoundland. However, in the Caribbean, Martinique, Guadeloupe, St. Lucia, and Marie-Galante were restored to France.

A few days after the signing of the treaty, Louis XV wrote, "The peace we have just reached is neither good nor glorious, as I am the first to admit. But given these regrettable circumstances, it is the best we could hope for [...]." The king and his ministers felt they had managed to safeguard the essential elements that would allow France to get back on its feet. In an attempt to brush over the country's defeat, the Court organized a host of activities in Paris and elsewhere across the country to celebrate peace, including balls, operas, and comedies. In Great Britain, while some were disappointed that part of the Caribbean islands were restored to France, the overall mood was triumphant. The Empire would now be able to further spread its influence and culture throughout the world.

The Future

In mid-May 1763, news of the signing of a peace treaty arrived in Canada. The *habitants* learned in posted proclamations that their colony was now officially a British possession. They were also informed of the clauses in the treaty that specifically concerned them, including the repayment of their debts by France. Great Britain, for its part, would allow those *habitants* who did not wish to become subjects of His Royal Majesty to sell their belongings and leave the country for the place of their choice. They were given eighteen months to do so. Those who remained would be allowed to practice their Roman Catholic religion insofar as such practice did not contravene British law. In the end, some 65,000 people chose to stay.

On October 7, 1763, George III enacted a royal proclamation to organize the governance of his new colonies in North America. In Canada, the districts of Québec, Trois-Rivières, and Montreal were combined to form the Province of Québec. James Murray was appointed governor, and was responsible for carrying out the instructions of the British government. By the end of the Seven Years' War and the vast restructuration that followed, Great Britain would possess one of the largest empires in modern history. □

7-12

7-12 On June 22, 1763, peace was celebrated in Paris with fireworks and the unveiling of an equestrian statue of King Louis XV.

To Stay or To Leave?

In the wake of the Capitulation of Montreal—and by extension, of New France—the *Canadiens* were exhausted from the long years of war that had left a trail of death, famine, and desolation. Moreover, their future was uncertain: the fate of their culture, institutions, and religion was to be decided by peace negotiations. The Treaty of Paris, which was signed February 10, 1763, officially made the *Canadiens* British subjects. For those who refused to switch allegiance, the treaty provided them 18 months to "retire with all safety and freedom wherever they shall think proper." While most of the seigneurs, members of the clergy, and *habitants* chose to stay, some 4,000 *Canadiens* preferred to leave, the majority of them to France. Those who left were nearly all members of the nobility and the elite, many of them administrators and traders who hoped to continue their careers in Europe. However, some of the emigrées struggled to make their way in France, and subsequently decided to return to Canada. ■

Chapter Eight
LEGACY

Remembering

The conquest of France's territories in North America, specifically the Battle of the Plains of Abraham on September 13, 1759, marked a tipping point, one extremely emotionally charged. While for the *Canadiens*, it signalled the beginning of a long rebuilding of their human and material resources, for the British authorities, it was a glorious victory that symbolized their supremacy, and they intended to make every effort to broadcast the event far and wide, to preserve its memory.

Their first initiative in this regard had to do with toponomy. Prior to the siege and capture of Québec, the "plains" or "heights" of Abraham referred to a chunk of land owned by the Ursuline nuns, but used by one Abraham Martin, who grazed his livestock there in the early 17th century. The locals were used to seeing Martin there, and eventually the site became associated with his first name. The designation didn't become official, however, until after the battle of September 13, 1759, when accounts, illustrations, maps, and drawings of the promontory of Québec began circulating, describing the conflict and disseminating far and wide the toponym *Plains of Abraham*.

In the wake of their victory, the British confiscated the land from the Ursulines owing to its strategic location. In 1802, they regulated the situation and officially leased the land from the nuns by way of an emphyteutic 100-year lease. On the battlefield,

only a single boulder rolled there by several British soldiers the day following the battle indicated the spot where Major General James Wolfe took his last breath. A friend of Wolfe's, Major Samuel Holland, who became a surveyor after the war, identified the location with a geodetic marker in 1790.

Aside from these individual initiatives, there was no immediate rush to officially commemorate the events. In the decades following the battle, geopolitical tensions ran high, and the site's strategic value eclipsed its historic significance. To avoid a repeat of the 1775 invasion that saw the "Americans" at Québec's doorstep, the British authorities erected a temporary citadel and four Martello towers on the Plains of Abraham to serve as a defensive line. After the War of 1812, the site remained under the control of the military and served as a field for manoeuvres and exercises by the garrison's soldiers.

Strangely, it wasn't on the Plains of Abraham that the battle of September 13, 1759, was first commemorated. Mindful of the fact the event was still a painful memory for some, albeit a glorious one for others, in the 1820s, Governor General Dalhousie took a conciliatory approach, commissioning an obelisk dedicated to both generals Wolfe and Montcalm. The monument was erected in Governors' Garden in September 1828, and bears an inscription in Latin (MORTEM. VIRTUS. COMMUNEM. FANAM. HISTORIA. MONUMENTUM. POSTERITAS. DEDIT.) that translates as "Their courage gave

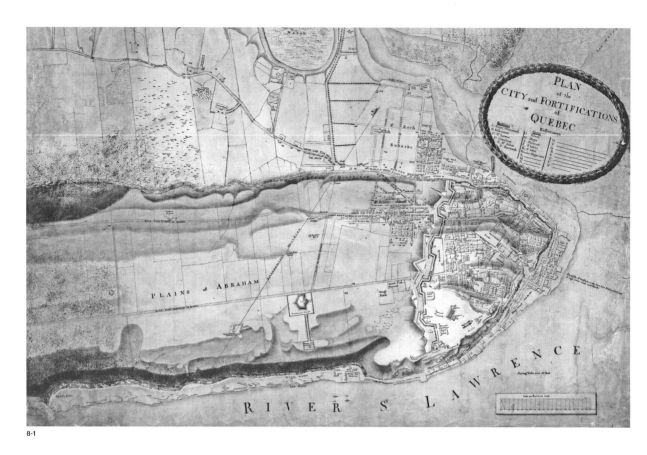

8-1

8-2

them a common death, history a common fame, posterity a common memorial."

However, part of the local British elite, those with stronger imperialist convictions, demanded a more glorious commemoration. In their view, Major General Wolfe was a true hero of the Empire, and as such, he deserved his own monument on the very site of his victory. After the events of 1759, many garrisoned soldiers and visitors would go to the site to pay their respects and collect a handful of what they considered consecrated soil. The Plains of Abraham had become a place people visited for its history.

In 1832, Governor General Aylmer responded to these increasingly vocal demands by having a truncated column erected on the spot where Holland's now-deteriorated marker stood. The monument bore the inscription "Here Died Wolfe Victorious." The Plains of Abraham became, for the British, an official site of patriotic veneration and pilgrimage. The monument's symbolic significance was so great that it eventually led to its demise, as it was not unusual for the many visitors to take away a piece of the column as a memento. In 1849, the column was replaced by a Doric column topped with a period helmet and bronze sword. This time, the monument was encircled by a forged iron fence with sharp stakes.

8-3

Les Braves

Also in 1849, workers unearthed bones and vestiges of weaponry near the presumed site of the Dumont Mill, located along Chemin Sainte-Foy, to the west of the Plains of Abraham. The mill had been the site of bitter fighting during the battle of April 28, 1760. Up until that point, that battle had been considered rather inconsequential, since it had failed to prevent the capitulation of the colony.

However, a detailed description of the clash emerged for the first time in 1848. Published in François-Xavier Garneau's *L'Histoire du Canada*, it shed new light on and lent greater significance to the battle. The colony, abandoned by France, had been forced to defend itself alone. The Chevalier de Lévis and his troops had showed great courage and succeeded in exacting revenge, with the French

8-2 On the right, Martello Tower 1 overlooks the St. Lawrence River. Martello towers were distinctive, coastal defensive structures that were in wide use in England in the 19th century. They had the advantage of being relatively inexpensive to build.

8-3 First monument dedicated to Major General James Wolfe in 1832 on the Plains of Abraham.

Army and the *Canadiens* vanquishing the British, but France's inertia and indifference rendered futile their efforts in Spring 1760 and sealed the fate of New France. The colony was lost, but her honour was saved.

The Société Saint-Jean-Baptiste in Québec undertook preliminary archeological digs during which bones were found and unearthed. In March 1854, it decided to organize a civic, religious, and military ceremony to transfer the remains, and launched a public campaign to have a monument erected. Just as Lévis's victory avenged Montcalm's defeat, so did the monument commemorating the Battle of Sainte-Foy aim to counterbalance the glorification of Wolfe.

During the ceremony on June 5, 1854, colonel and politician Étienne-Paschal Taché gave a speech. According to him, enough time had passed and, as in Europe, the days of discord were over: "England and France, centuries-old enemies, are now united by a close alliance […]. Shall we—descendants of these two great peoples—be the only ones to remain on the sidelines of this admirable movement? No, we shall forget our old quarrels, what some have called 'wars of race.' From this moment onwards, we shall form a single people—the Canadian people—a people that, while perhaps not homogenous, is certainly united by heart and sentiment."

With great solemnity, the remains of both victors and vanquished were combined and buried together on the battlefield, next to the presumed vestiges of the Dumont Mill. Not all, however, approved of the ceremony, and French-Canadian nationalists and imperialists alike were quick to voice their opposition. Member of parliament Louis-Joseph Papineau summed up the unease in the two camps: "Holding a single celebration for those who died defending their nationality and those who died attempting to impose their own strikes me as bizarre and nonsensical, not to mention abject flattery."

In July 1855, the city of Québec was buzzing with excitement. The French warship *La Capricieuse*, the

8-4

first French Navy ship to arrive in Canada since the demise of the colony, had just docked. The event was celebrated in grandiose fashion by the local population. The laying of the cornerstone of the Des Braves Monument, where the soldiers' remains had been buried the previous year, was one of the celebratory activities, and provided an opportunity to reaffirm the message of conciliation and fusion. But it wasn't until October 19, 1863, that the work was completed and inaugurated. The monument donated by Prince Jérôme-Napoléon consisted of a column topped by a statue of Bellona, the Roman goddess of war.

Preserving the Plains

In 1871, the last British troops withdrew from Canada, signalling the end of the army's hold over the land on the Plains of Abraham. The Canadian Government took over from the British authorities as manager of the site, and was quickly subjected to public pressure. The lease between the government and the Ursuline religious order was set to expire in 1902, and some feared the nuns would decide to subdivide the land into lots. Aware of the site's historic and symbolic value, dignitaries and regular citizens alike demanded that the federal authorities intervene, and their pleas made headlines in the newspapers across Canada.

At the same time, a worldwide trend had made its way to Québec. Like many European cities that were opening their royal gardens to the public, and a number of American cities that were setting aside and planning green spaces, Québec wanted to create its own large public park. Urban parks were all the rage in the 19th century, and the provincial capital was no stranger to the movement that sought to combine access to nature with opportunities for good health and well-being. The Plains of Abraham, with their ideal location and huge expanse, were the perfect spot.

In the final decade of the 19th century, the movement to preserve the Plains of Abraham gained ground. In 1899, the Literary and Historical Society of Quebec launched a campaign to protect the site and, on September 20, 1901, its efforts paid off. After lengthy negotiations, the Government of

8-5

8-4 On June 5, 1854, the remains of the French and British soldiers killed in the battle on April 28, 1760, were transported in a funeral carriage to the Québec Basilica, where mass was celebrated for the deceased. Following the service, the remains were buried on the battlefield.

8-5 Bellona, Goddess of War, stands atop the Des Braves Monument. She is holding a lance and shield, and faces the part of the battlefield that was occupied by the French Army on April 28, 1760.

8-6

Canada agreed to purchase the Plains of Abraham from the Ursuline order for the sum of $80,000, although it was evaluated at $138,000. It also undertook to convert the Plains of Abraham into a public park. The day of the transaction, the site was handed over to the City of Québec by way of an emphyteutic lease. While some trees were planted and a few paths laid out, the future and vocation of the site were still uncertain, and in 1905, a municipal committee even went so far as to question the relevance of turning the Plains into a park.

Grey's Quest

When he arrived in Canada in December 1904, the new governor general, Lord Grey, was well aware that a difficult task awaited him, as Canada's participation in the Boer War in South Africa (1899–1902) had sparked a crisis within government and created deep divisions between French and English Canadians. Grey's mandate was to reconcile Canadians from all backgrounds and to bring them into the fold of the Empire. He soon realized that to promote this unity, he would have to play the emotional card. And so, the quest began for a national symbol.

On his first visit to Québec City, in the summer of 1905, Grey decided that the plan introduced by one of his predecessors, Lord Dufferin, to beautify the city should be carried through to fruition. The city's historic sites were in a state of disrepair, including the Plains of Abraham, which were under threat from urbanization. Consequently, his quest took on new meaning: he would restore the prestige of that sacred land and transform it into a symbol that would transcend their differences and unite all French and English Canadians.

The upcoming 300th anniversary of the City of Québec, in 1908, helped inject momentum into the process. The city's mayor, George Garneau, created a commission to advise on the subject and nature of the tricentennial celebrations. In its first report, released in 1906, the commission recommended creating a park that would stretch from the walls of the Citadel all the way to the Ursuline nuns' property, acquired in 1901, and including the Des Braves Monument on Chemin Sainte-Foy. That way, the sites of both battles of Québec would be preserved.

At the same time as the commission was carrying out its work, others lobbied Canada's Prime Minister, Sir Wilfrid Laurier. Laurier, however, was hesitant to act. Not only did the project represent a financial burden for the Canadian economy, which was still on shaky ground; it also had the potential to sow more discontent between nationalists and imperialists. Lord Grey was aware his undertaking had touched a nerve, and he chose to revisit his position. To provide Canada with a shared vision, he needed to recognize defeat without conceding victory. By elevating the battle of April 28, 1760, to the same level as the September 13, 1759, battle, and including the Sainte-Foy battlefield in the planned park, he would be commemorating the heroic conduct of the armies of the two founding peoples.

Lord Grey's vision, needless to say, failed to garner unanimous support among the French-speaking nationalist elite, and was openly denounced by its more radical members, whose views were summed up by journalist Paul Tardivel: "We shall have not a celebration of Catholic Canada, not a celebration of Québec, but a celebration of the *grand tout canadien*; a celebration of the Empire. It is not the founding of Québec they want to celebrate; it is the capture of Québec by the English. It is not the exploit of Champlain; it is the exploit of Wolfe."

Exasperated by Tardivel's crusade, which continued to gain traction, the organizers of the tricentennial celebrations began to fear the negative impact it might have on the event. One of the key promoters of the project, renowned journalist and historian Thomas Chapais, capitalizing on his prestige, adopted a reassuring tone, promising that the tricentennial celebrations would mark not only the birth of the city, but also its growth. On the subject of the Plains of Abraham, he wrote: "The project put forth by His Excellency the Governor General does not seek to take the Plains of Abraham away from us, nor to change its historic name, nor to offend our

8-8

8-7

8-6 The Plains of Abraham circa 1908. In the middle of the picture, one can see Martello Tower 1, the prison, and the Québec Observatory.

8-7 Albert Henry George Grey, 4th Earl Grey, was Canada's governor general from 1904 to 1911.

8-8 The site of the battle of April 28, 1760, was spared from urbanization just in the nick of time. In 1908, nearly the entire area had been subdivided into lots, and two buildings had already been erected. All of the land was acquired between 1910 and 1912 by the National Battlefields Commission to create and develop Des Braves Park.

rightful sensitivities [...]. The Plains of Abraham shall remain the Plains of Abraham; they shall not be stolen from us; their name shall not be removed [...]; the memories they inspire can never be destroyed or altered. On the contrary, they shall be perpetuated in bronze and marble."

Despite the tensions, Lord Grey forged ahead with his plans, although he soon realized that the costs associated with his beautification program and the park's creation would amount to nearly $2 million. Since the federal, provincial, and municipal authorities did not have the means to cover the costs on their own, Grey launched a fundraising campaign and solicited contributions from the other provinces as well as from groups across the country and the Empire. However, the federal government's reluctance to invest in the project hampered the fundraising efforts. Grey was unable to spark the interest of the Empire or Canada's financial community. In the end, the governor general's campaign was only partially successful. Of his $2 million target, he managed to raise only one-quarter of that amount.

Nonetheless, in the early months of 1908, the pieces of the puzzle all began to fall into place. Prime Minister Laurier eventually gave in and, at the last minute, granted $300,000 for the upcoming commemorations. This was in addition to the $100,000 contributed by the provinces of Québec and Ontario, as well as the additional amounts Grey had managed to raise. By the same token, Laurier created the National Battlefields Commission. It was chaired by the mayor of Québec City, George Garneau, and was tasked with managing the funds and organizing the city's tricentennial celebrations.

Creating a Park and Perpetuating the Heritage

Québec City's tricentennial celebrations stretched over two weeks, from July 19 to 31, and were a resounding success. The National Battlefields Commission had achieved its first goal. Its next task was to acquire and preserve the city's great historic battlefields, restore them insofar as possible to their original condition, and convert them into a national park.

8-9

8-9 George Garneau was mayor of Québec City from 1906 to 1910, and chaired the National Battlefields Commission from 1908 to 1939.

Parade of Honour

On the occasion of the tricentennial celebrations of the City of Québec in July
1908, the Plains of Abraham served as the
backdrop for a series of grand pageants in
which the history of the city was played out
through eight themes in thirteen tableaux.
The final event consisted of an impressive
and hugely popular parade of honour fea-
turing costumed extras marching as soldiers of the Marquis de Montcalm and of
Major General Wolfe. At the end of the
parade, which was attended by the Prince
of Wales, the two "armies" marched to the
Wolfe Monument, where they laid wreaths
bearing the inscription *Honour to Wolfe* and
Honour to Montcalm. ■

8-10A

8-10B

8-10A Extras in the army of
the Marquis de Montcalm.

8-10B Extras in the army of
Major General Wolfe.

With the sum of $550,000 raised by Governor General Grey, the National Battlefields Commission was now ready to acquire the land, remove the buildings that were an eyesore on the grounds, and draw up a development plan for the site in its entirety. In 1909, it hired landscape architect Frederick G. Todd, who described the site in glowing terms:

> *With a situation unequalled and historical associations almost unparalleled, it is clear that you have in this property, where the fate of Canada and perhaps the whole continent more than once hung in the balance, the making of a park "par excellence." There are other parks of magnificent views [...], but it is no exaggeration to say that in no other place can we find such grandeur of proportion, such sublime views combined with such a wealth of historical associations, as is encompassed within this park [...].*

It took approximately fifty years for the National Battlefields Commission to complete the work required to preserve the Plains of Abraham and the Des Braves Park and create the 103-hectare Battlefields Park. Over the course of the 20th century, the space took shape, asserting its dual vocation as both an urban park and historic site. Commemorative elements were erected highlighting the events of 1759 and 1760, albeit in a discreet and sober fashion. In 1913, the restoration of the Wolfe Monument echoed the inauguration in 1911 of a monument dedicated to the Marquis de Montcalm near the park.

Nevertheless, even years later, the emotionally charged significance of the battles of 1759 and 1760 and the Plains of Abraham still lingers, as witnessed by the destruction of the Wolfe Monument in 1963 (an act attributed to the Front de libération du Québec) and the intense controversy sparked by the commemoration of the 250th anniversary of the Battle of the Plains of Abraham in 2009. The Seven Years' War marked a pivotal point in North America, resulting, among other consequences, in the end of the French Regime in Canada. The Plains of Abraham, theatre of the war's most decisive episodes, are forever associated with that troubled period that redefined borders and marked generations. □

8-11

8-12

8-13

8-11 In his landscaping plan for the Battlefields Park, Frederick G. Todd divided the grounds into five main zones, setting out space for plantations, with avenues and walkways that followed the contours of the land, monumental park entrances, and historical vestiges that were preserved and showcased.

8-12 The Wolfe Monument, four years prior to its restoration in 1913.

8-13 Silhouettes dotted along the Plains of Abraham Trail are a reminder of the efforts of the British soldiers as they struggled to scale the cliffs of Cap Diamant in the early hours of September 13, 1759.

139

an mil sept cens cinquante-neuf le quator

nois de Septembre a été inhumé dans l'Égl

religieuse Ursulines de Québec haut et puissan

uis-Joseph Marquis de Montcalm Lieutena

armées du Roy, Commandeur de l'Ordre

ilitaire de St Louis, Commandant en Chef

terre en l'Amérique Septentrionale, decede

u de ses blessures au combat de la veille,

Sacrements qu'il a reçus avec beaucoup

de Religion. Etoient presents à son in

Resche, Cugnet et Collet Chanoines

thédrale, Mr de Ramezay Commanda

cc et tout le corps des Officiers. Resche

Collet chne

ACADEMIC DICTIONARIES AND ENCYLOPEDIAS, Wikipedia, "Wolfe's Manifesto" (accessed January 6, 2022) [online] https://en-academic.com/dic.nsf/enwiki/892048.

ANDERSON, Fred. *Crucible of War: The Seven Years' War and the Fate of Empire in British North America, 1754-1766*, New York: Alfred Knopf, 2000.

BOUGAINVILLE, Louis-Antoine de. Écrits sur le Canada. Mémoires, journal, lettres, Sillery: Septentrion, 2003.

BRUMWELL, Stephen. *Redcoats: The British Soldier and War in the Americas, 1755-1763*, Cambridge: Cambridge University Press, 2002.

CASGRAIN, abbé Henri-Raymond (dir.). *Journal des campagnes du Chevalier de Lévis en Canada de 1756-1760*, Montréal: C. O. Beauchemin et Fils, coll. "Manuscrits du maréchal de Lévis," 1889.

—, *Journal du marquis de Montcalm durant ses campagnes en Canada de 1756 à 1759*, Québec: Imprimerie L.-J. Demers, coll. "Manuscrits du maréchal de Lévis," 1895.

—, *Lettres de divers particuliers au chevalier de Lévis*, Québec: Imprimerie L.-J. Demers & Frère, coll. "Manuscrits du maréchal de Lévis," 1895.

—, *Lettres de la cour de Versailles au baron de Dieskau, au marquis de Montcalm et au chevalier de Lévis*, Québec: Imprimerie L.-J. Demers & Frère, coll. "Manuscrits du maréchal de Lévis," 1890.

—, *Lettres de l'intendant Bigot au chevalier de Lévis*, Québec: Imprimerie L.-J. Demers & Frère, coll. "Manuscrits du maréchal de Lévis," 1895.

—, *Lettres de M. de Bourlamaque au maréchal de Lévis*, Québec: Imprimerie L.-J. Demers & Frère, coll. "Manuscrits du maréchal de Lévis," 1891.

—, *Lettres du chevalier de Lévis concernant la guerre du Canada (1756-1760)*, Montréal: C.O. Beauchemin & Fils, coll. "Manuscrits du maréchal de Lévis," 1889.

—, *Lettres du marquis de Montcalm au chevalier de Lévis*, Québec: Imprimerie L.-J. Demers & Frère, coll. "Manuscrits du maréchal de Lévis," 1894.

—, *Lettres du marquis de Vaudreuil au chevalier de Lévis*, Québec: Imprimerie L.-J. Demers & Frère, coll. "Manuscrits du maréchal de Lévis," 1895.

—, *Lettres et pièces militaires, instructions, ordres, mémoires, plans de campagne et de défense, 1756-1760*, Québec: Imprimerie L.-J. Demers & Frère, coll. "Manuscrits du maréchal de Lévis," 1891.

A Collection of the Acts Passed in the Parliament of Great Britain and of Other Public Acts Relative to Canada, Québec: P. E. Desbarats, 1800.

DECHÊNE, Louise (trans. Peter Feldstein). *People, State, and War Under the French Regime in Canada*, Montreal and Kingston: McGill-Queens University Press, 2021.

DELÂGE, Denys. "Les Premières Nations et la Guerre de la Conquête (1754-1765)," *Les Cahiers des dix*, no. 63, 2009, p. 1-67.

DOUGHTY, Arthur and George W. PARMELEE. *The Siege of Quebec and the Battle of the Plains of Abraham*, Québec: Dussault and Proulx, 1901, 6 volumes.

DULL, Jonathan R. *La Guerre de Sept Ans. Histoire navale, politique et diplomatique*, Bécherel (France): Les Perséides, 2009.

DZIEMBOWSKI, Edmond. *La Guerre de Sept Ans, 1756-1763*, Québec: Septentrion, 2015.

—, *Les Pitt. L'Angleterre face à la France, 1708-1806*, Québec: Septentrion, 2015.

FONK, Bertrand and Laurent VEYSSIÈRE (dir.). *La Fin de la Nouvelle-France*, Paris: Armand Colin et Ministère de la Défense, 2013.

FRASER, Malcolm. *Extract from a Manuscript Journal, Relating to the Siege of Quebec in 1759*, Québec: Literary and Historical Society of Quebec, 1867.

FRÉGAULT, Guy. *La Guerre de la Conquête, 1754-1760*, Montréal: Fides, 2011 [1955].

GARNEAU, François-Xavier. *Histoire du Canada depuis sa découverte jusqu'à nos jours. Tome second*, Québec: P. Lamoureux, 1859 [1848].

GRENIER, Fernand (ed.). *Papiers Contrecoeur et autres documents concernant le conflit anglo-français sur l'Ohio de 1745 à 1756*, Québec: Presses de l'Université Laval, 1952.

GROULX, Patrice. "La commémoration de la bataille de Sainte-Foy. Du discours de la loyauté à la 'fusion des races'," *Revue d'histoire de l'Amérique française*, vol. 55, no. 1, 2001, p. 45-83.

IMBEAULT, Sophie, VAUGEOIS, Denis and VEYSSIÈRE, Laurent. 1763. *Le traité de Paris bouleverse l'Amérique*, Québec: Septentrion, 2013.

INTERNET ARCHIVE. "Full text of Governor Murray's Journal of Quebec, from 18th September, 1759, to 25th May, 1760." (accessed December 3, 2021) [online] https://archive.org/stream/governormurraysj00murr/governormurraysj00murr_djvu.txt.

JACKSON, Donald (dir.). *The Diaries of George Washington*, vol. 1: *1748-65*, Charlottesville: University Press of Virginia, 1976.

The Journal of Jeffery Amherst, Recording the Military Career of General Amherst in America from 1758 to 1763, Toronto/ Chicago: The Ryerson Press and University of Chicago Press, 1931.

KNOX, John. *An Historical Journal of the Campaigns in North-America for the Years 1757, 1758, 1759 and 1760*, London: W. Johnston and J. Dodsley, 1769.

LACOURSIÈRE, Jacques and QUIMPER, Hélène. *Québec ville assiégée, 1759-1760. D'après les acteurs et les témoins*, Québec: Septentrion, 2009.

LA PAUSE, Charles de Plantavit de Margon de. *Mémoires et papiers du chevalier de la Pause, 1755-1760*, Québec: Imprimerie de la Reine, s.d.

MACLEOD, Peter. *Northern Armageddon: The Battle of the Plains of Abraham*, Vancouver: Douglas & McIntyre, 2008.

–, *Backs to the Wall: The Battle of Sainte-Foy and the Conquest of Canada*, Vancouver: Douglas and McIntyre, 2016.

MALARTIC, Anne-Joseph-Hyppolyte de Maurès de. *Journal des campagnes au Canada de 1755 à 1760*, Dijon: L. Damidot, 1890.

MANNING, Stephen. *Quebec: The Story of Three Sieges, A Military History*, London: Continuum, 2009.

MURRAY, James. *Journal of the Siege of Quebec, 1760*, Québec: Middleton & Dawson, 1871.

NATIONAL PARK SERVICE. "Fort Necessity National Battlefield Pennsylvania, Articles of Capitulation" (accessed September 27, 2021) [online] https://www.nps.gov/fone/learn/historyculture/capitulation.htm.

NELLES, H. V. *The Art of Nation-Building: Pageantry and Spectacle at Quebec's Tercentenary*, Toronto: University of Toronto Press, 1999.

NOËL, Dave. *Montcalm, général américain*, Montréal: Boréal, 2018.

Œuvres complètes de Voltaire. Tome vingt-neuvième, Paris: Librairie L. Hachette et Cie, 1861.

PANET, Jean-Claude. *Journal du Siège de Québec en 1759*, Montréal: Eusèbe Sénécal imprimeur-éditeur, 1866.

PRIMARYDOCUMENTS.CA. "Treaty of Paris, 10 February 1763" (accessed December 24, 2021) [online] https://primarydocuments.ca/the-treaty-of-paris-1763/.

La Prise de Québec / The Taking of Quebec, 1759-1760, Québec: Commission des champs de bataille nationaux (National Battlefields Commission) and Musée national des beaux-arts du Québec, 2009.

Report by Frederick G. Todd, landscape architect, November 15, 1909, Archives of the National Battlefields Commission.

RAMEZAY, Jean-Baptiste-Nicolas-Roch de. *Mémoires du Sieur de Ramezay, commandant à Québec, au sujet de la reddition de cette ville, le 18 septembre 1759*, Québec: Presses Lovell, 1861.

RÉCHER, abbé Jean-Félix. *Journal du siège de Québec en 1759*, Québec: Société historique de Québec, 1959.

Relation de ce qui s'est passé au siège de Québec et de la prise du Canada par une religieuse de l'Hôpital général de Québec, Québec: Mercury, 1855.

SOLON LAW ARCHIVE. "Articles of Capitulation of Montreal" (accessed January 9, 2022) [online] https://www.solon.org/Constitutions/Canada/English/PreConfederation/cap_montreal.html#1.

SOLON LAW ARCHIVE. "Placard from his Excellency General Amherst" (accessed January 9, 2022) [online] https://www.solon.org/Constitutions/Canada/English/PreConfederation/placard_17600922.html.

STACEY, C. P. *Québec, 1759. The Siege and the Battle*, Toronto: Robin Brass Studio Inc., 2002 (revised edition)

TERJANIAN, Anoush F., *Commerce and its Discontents in Eighteenth-Century French Political Thought*, Cambridge: Cambridge University Press, 2012.

THOMPSON, James. *A Short Authentic Account of the Expedition Against Quebec in the Year 1759, Under Command of Major General James Wolfe by a Volunteer upon that Expedition*, Québec: Middleton & Dawson, 1872.

VEYSSIÈRE, Laurent (dir.). *La Nouvelle-France en héritage*, Paris: Armand Colin and Ministère de la Défense, 2013.

VEYSSIÈRE, Laurent and FONK, Bertrand (dir.). *La Guerre de Sept Ans en Nouvelle-France*, Québec: Septentrion, 2011.

VIRGINIA MUSEUM OF HISTORY AND CULTURE. "Céleron Plate" (accessed January 4, 2022) [online] https://virginiahistory.org/learn/celeron-plate.

WEAPONS AND WARFARE, History and Hardware of Warfare, "The Plains of Abraham II" (accessed January 14, 2022) [online] https://weaponsandwarfare.com/2020/02/11/the-plains-of-abraham-ii/

WILLSON, Beckles. *The Life and Letters of James Wolfe*, New York: Dodd Mead & Company, 1909.

ILLUSTRATION AND PHOTO CREDITS

ABBREVIATIONS

ADQ   Archives du diocèse de Québec

AGSA   Art Gallery of South Australia

ANBC   Archives of the National Battlefields Commission

ASP   Alamy Stock Photo

BAnQ   Bibliothèque et Archives nationales du Québec

BDR   Brown Digital Repository, Brown University Library

BI   Bridgeman Images

CCQ   Centre de conservation du Québec

CWM   Canadian War Museum

JCBL   John Carter Brown Library, Brown University

LAC   Library and Archives Canada

LC   Library of Congress (USA)

MA   Monastère des Augustines

MAEDI   Ministère des Affaires étrangères et du Développement international (France)

MC   Musée de la civilisation

McCM   McCord Museum, Montreal Social History Museum

MNBAQ   Musée national des beaux-arts du Québec

MR22eR   Musée Royal 22e Régiment

MWLU   Museums, Washington and Lee University

NAC   National Archives Catalog (USA)

NCMA   North Carolina Museum of Art

NGC   National Gallery of Canada

NMM   National Maritime Museum (UK)

NPG   National Portrait Gallery (UK)

NYPLDC   New York Public Library Digital Collections

PC   Parks Canada

PCMU   Pôle culturel du monastère des Ursulines

SM   Stewart Museum

UBC   University of British Columbia

UC   University of Chicago

VMHC   Virginia Museum of History & Culture

WAM   Walters Art Museum (USA)

WHS   Wisconsin Historical Society

FRONT COVER

C   *La Bataille des plaines d'Abraham*, Charles Huot, circa 1902. MR22eR. 1983 105, 001.

INTRODUCTION

I   *Vue générale de Québec depuis la pointe Lévis* (detail). BAC. 1989-286-2. 2898089.

CHAPTER ONE

1-0   *Carte d'une partie de l'Amérique septentrionale*, Commissioners for adjusting the boundaries of the British and French possessions in America, 1755. BAnQ. 2663565.

1-1   *Louis XV*, Louis Michel van Loo (1707-1771). Bibliothèque municipale, Versailles, France. RT384477. RMN-Grand Palais / Art Resource, New York.

1-2   *King George II*, Thomas Hudson, 1744. Oil on canvas. NPG, London. NPG 670.

1-3   *Carte de l'Amérique septentrionale depuis le 28 degré de latitude jusqu'au 72*, Jacques Nicolas Bellin, 1755. BAnQ. 3670685.

1-4   Image from Henri-Louis Duhamel du Monceau. *Traité général des pesches*, Paris: Chez Saillant & Nyon, libraires, rue Saint-Jean-de-Beauvais, and Chez Desaint, libraire, rue du Foin-Saint-Jacques, 1782, Part 2, section 1, panel 17.B. UBC.

1-5   *Miliciens canadiens*, Francis Back. PC.

1-6   *A View of Charlestown, Now Charleston, South Carolina, United States of America in the 18th Century*. Classic Image / ASP.

1-7   *Partie de l'Amérique septentrionale, qui comprend le cours de l'Ohio, la Nlle Angleterre, la Nlle York, le New Jersey, la Pennsylvanie, le Maryland, la Virginie, la Caroline*, Gilles Robert de Vaugondy, 1755. BAnQ. 2663645.

1-8   *George Washington's Map, Accompanying His "Journal to the Ohio,"* George Washington, [Boston, 1754]. LC. 99446116.

1-9   *Lead Marker, Céleron Plate*, 1749. VMHC. 1849.1.

1-10 *Ohio River, 7 Miles Above Madison, La,* 1853. Manuscripts and Archives Division, The New York Public Library. NYPLDC.

1-11 *Military Commission Granted to Chief Okana-Stoté of the Cherokee by Governor Louis Billouart, Chevalier de Kerlérec* (detail). Department of State, Office of the Secretary. NAC. 6924937.

1-12 *George Washington as Colonel of the Virginia Regiment,* Charles Willson Peale, 1772. Courtesy of MWLU. U1897.1.1.

1-13 *Assassinat de Jumonville au fort de la Nécessité,* image from Alexandre Dumas, *La Régence et Louis Quinze,* Paris: Malmenayde et de Riberolles, 1855, p. 281.

1-14 *Britain's Rights Maintaind; or French Ambition Dismantled,* 1755. Courtesy of JCBL.

1-15 *Pierre de Rigaud de Vaudreuil de Cavagnial, marquis de Vaudreuil (1698-1778).* LAC. R3938-1. 2895086.

1-16 *The Capture of the "Alcide" and "Lys," 8 June 1755.* NMM, Greenwich, London, Caird Collection. BHC0376.

CHAPTER TWO

2-0 *Braddock's Defeat* (detail), Edwin Willard Deming. WHS. ID 1900.

2-1 *British General Edward Braddock Marching Through Wilderness to Fort Duquesne Pennsylvania in the French and Indian War,* 1755. North Wind Picture Archives / ASP.

2-2 *A Sketch of the Field of Battle With the Disposition of the Troops in the Beginning of the Engagement of the 9th of July on the Monongahela 7 Miles from Fort Du Quesne,* [1755]. LC. Map, gm71002313.

2-3 *Alliance de l'Autriche et de la France,* Jeanne-Antoinette Poisson, marquise de Pompadour, 1756. WAM. 92.548.60.

2-4 *Braddock's Defeat,* Edwin Willard Deming. WHS. ID 1900.

2-5 *The English Lion Dismember'd: Or, the Voice of the Public for an Enquiry Into the Loss of Minorca— With Adl: B--g's Plea Before His Examiners,* 1756. Prints, Drawings and Watercolors from the Anne S. K. Brown Military Collection. BDR.

2-6 *Louis-Joseph, marquis de Montcalm.* LAC. 1991-209-1. C027665.

2-7 *French General Louis-Joseph de Montcalm, 1712-1759. Here Seen Trying to Stop His Native American Allies From Killing British Soldiers and Civilians Who Had Surrendered After the Battle of Fort William Henry During the French and Indian War, 1754-1763.* Classic Image / ASP.

2-8 *William Pitt, Later First Earl of Chatham (1708–1778),* William Hoare, circa 1754. Oil on canvas. 50 1/16 in. × 40 1/16 in. (127.2 cm × 101.8 cm). Gift from Mr. and Mrs. Aubrey Lee Brooks. NCMA, Raleigh.

2-9 *Louis-Charles-Auguste Fouquet, maréchal-duc de Belle-Isle (1684-1761),* Maurice-Quentin de La Tour (1704-1788). Institut de France, Paris, France. RMN-Grand Palais / Art Resource, NY. ART597829.

2-10 *A View of the Bay of Gaspe, in the Government of Quebec, Situate in the Gulf of St. Lawrence,* excerpt from *Gentleman's Magazine,* between 1760 and 1800, unknown, after a drawing by Hervey Smyth. Etching and watercolour highlights, 19 cm × 26.7 cm (paper); 15.5 cm × 24.4 cm (image). Photo credit: MNBAQ, Idra Labrie. MNBAQ. Purchase. 1954.05.

2-11 *Sir Jeffery Amherst.* LAC. 1958-214-1. 2837548.

2-12 *British Resentment or the French Fairly Coopt at Louisbourg,* 1755. Courtesy of JCLB.

CHAPTER THREE

3-0 *A Plan of Québec and Environs, With Its Defences and... During the Siege of That Place in 1759* (detail), Joseph F.W. Des Barres, [1780]. BAnQ. 2663540.

3-1 *Antoine, Louis comte de Bougainville.* LAC. 1989-518-4. 2895779.

3-2 *Nicolas-René Berryer.* Hansrad Collection / ASP.

3-3 *Mandement de Mgr Henri-Marie Dubreil de Pontbriand à l'occasion de la guerre. Imprimé,* Québec, *Mandements,* vol. 1, p. 87, 1758. ADQ. AAQ, 10 A.

3-4 *Vue générale de Québec depuis la pointe Lévis.* LAC. 1989-286-2. 2898089.

3-5 *James Wolfe.* LAC. 1995-134-1. 2894990.

3-6 *Sir Charles Saunders, 1713-1775.* LAC. 1970-188-50. 2873809.

3-7 *Landing of the British Troops at Quebec, 1759,* William Elliott (*fl.* 1774-1792), 1790. Oil on canvas. Gift from Frank L. Babbott (Class of 1878). Mead Art Museum / BI.

3-8 *Annales du monastère des Ursulines de Québec*, tome 1: *1639-1822*. PCMU, Fonds Monastère des Ursulines de Québec. MQ/1E/1/1/3,2.1.

3-9 *Plan de la ville de Québec capitale du Canada en Amérique du Nord*. LAC. 4160245.

3-10 *A New Chart of the River St. Laurence, From the Island of Anticosti to the Falls of Richelieu: With All the Islands, Rocks, Shoals, and Soundings, Also Particular Directions for Navigating the River With Safety, Taken by the Order of Charles Saunders, Esqr. in the Expedition Against Quebec in 1759* (detail), Jeffery Thomas (-1771), [London, 1760]. LC. Map. 74696159.

3-11 *Premier manifeste du Général Wolfe affiché à la porte de l'église de Beaumont*, signed by Wolfe. BAnQ. 03Q,P224,P2_01.

3-12 *Artillerie*, image from Guillaume Le Blond, *Traité de l'artillerie, ou des Armes et machines en usage à la guerre, depuis l'invention de la poudre*, Paris: Charles-Antoine Jombert, 1743, panel 5.

3-13 *French Fire Attacking the British Fleet off Quebec, 28 June 1759*. NMM, Greenwich, London, Caird Collection. BHC0393.

3-14 *A Song by Genl. Wolf (1759)*. Prints, Drawings and Watercolors from the Anne S. K. Brown Military Collection. BDR. 228576.

3-15 *A Bombardment*, image from *Théorie nouvelle sur le Mécanisme de l'Artillerie*, Paris, 1741. British Library Board, All Rights Reserved / BI.

3-16 *A View of the Bishop's House and the Ruin as they appear in going up the Hill from the Lower to the Upper Town*, LAC. 1989-283-11. 2895060.

3-17 *A View of the Fall of Montmorency and the Attack made by General Wolfe on the French Intrenchments near Beauport, with the Grenadiers of the Army*, engraved by William Elliot, drawn by Hervey Smyth, 1760. Etching and burin, 46.3 cm × 62.8 cm (paper); 36.4 cm × 53 cm (panel); 33.4 cm × 51.7 cm (image). Photo credit: MNBAQ, Patrick Altman. MNBAQ, Donated by Archives de la province de Québec. 1967.214.

3-18 *A View of the City of Quebec with the Cittadel and Outworks on Cape Diamond*. LAC. 1989-221-2. 2895101.

3-19 *George Townshend, 4th Viscount and 1st Marquess Townshend*, Samuel William Reynolds, published by Hodgson & Graves, after Sir Joshua Reynolds (1759-1761), 1838. mezzotint. NPG, London. NPG D14345.

3-20 *Le Général James Wolfe à Québec, 1759*, George Townshend. McCord Museum. M1791.

CHAPTER FOUR

4-0 *Scaling of the Heights of Abraham* (detail), Richard Caton Woodville (1825-1855). Look and Learn / BI.

4-1 *Débarquement de troupes chez l'ennemi*, image from Nicolas-Marie Ozanne, *Marine militaire ou Recueil des differens vaisseaux qui servent à la guerre, suivis des Manœuvres qui ont le plus de raport au combat ainsi qua l'ataque et la deffense des ports*, Paris, Chez Chereau, [17--], panel 47.

4-2 *Plan de la ville de Québec capitale du Canada en Amérique du Nord* (detail). LAC. 4160245.

4-3 *View of the Siege of Quebec*, 1780. Prints, Drawings and Watercolors from the Anne S. K. Brown Military Collection. BDR.

4-4 *View of the Landing Place above the Town of Quebec* (detail). LAC. 1997-3-2, 2837444.

4-5 *Scaling of the Heights of Abraham*, Richard Caton Woodville (1825-1855). Look and Learn / BI.

4-6 *English Soldiers Scaling the Heights of Abraham, 1759*, Frank Otis Small, 1903. Prints, Drawings and Watercolors from the Anne S. K. Brown Military Collection. BDR.

4-7 *Les Plaines d'Abraham, Québec*, George Heriot, circa 1795. Watercolour and ink on card, 21.5 cm × 32.5 cm. Photographer: MNBAQ, Patrick Altman. MNBAQ. Purchase. 1987.34.

4-8 *La Bataille des plaines d'Abraham*, Charles Huot, circa 1902. MR22eR. 1983 105, 001.

4-9 *Plan of the Action on the Heights of Abraham Near Quebec. Septr. 13th: 1759*. Courtesy of JCBL. 66-109.

4-10 *Représentation du lieu de tir, au-dessus de la ville de Québec, on y voit l'assaut de l'ennemi, 13 septembre 1759*. LAC. 1997-220-1. 2895905.

4-11 *Art militaire, exercice, planche III*, image from Denis Diderot and Jean Le Rond d'Alembert, *Encyclopédie ou Dictionnaire raisonné des sciences et des arts et des métiers*, ARTFL Encyclopédie project. UC.

7-2 *A Particular Map to Illustrate Gen. Amherst's Expedition to Montreal With a Plan of the Town & Draught of Ye Island*, J. Gibson, *Gentleman's magazine*, [1760]. BAnQ. 2663121.

7-3 *Traité et conventions, pour les malades, blessés & prisonniers de guerre des troupes de terre de Sa Majesté très-chrétienne & de Sa Majesté britannique*, 1759. SM. S001/A2.3,8.7.

7-4 *Passage of Amherst's Army down the Rapids of the St. Lawrence toward Montreal*, LAC. 1948-13-1. 2895342.

7-5 *Plan of the Town and Fortifications of Montreal or Ville Marie in Canada*, 1759. BAnQ. 5084773.

7-6 *La Capitulation de Montréal*, 1760, image from *Nos racines, l'histoire vivante des Québécois*, No. 27, "La colonie capitula." Les Éditions Transmo, 1979, p. 538.

7-7 *French General Louis-Joseph de Montcalm, 1712-1759. Here Seen Trying to Stop His Native American Allies From Killing British Soldiers and Civilians Who Had Surrendered After the Battle of Fort William Henry During the French and Indian War, 1754-1763* (detail). Classic Image / ASP.

7-8 *The Charity of General Amherst*, Francis Hayman. CWM, Beaverbrook Collection of Military Art. CWM 19940037-001.

7-9 *King George III in Coronation Robe*. AGSA. 0.561.

7-10 *Traité définitif de paix entre le Roi, le Roi de la Grande Bretagne et le Roi d'Espagne, signé à Paris le 10 février 1763*. MAEDI, France. TRA 17630001/001/035.

7-11 *Paix rendue à l'Europe*, Jean-Baptiste Tilliard, 1763. Rijksmuseum. RP-P-1928-204.

7-12 *Décoration du feu d'artifice tiré à Londres en réjouissance de la paix en 1763*, Mondhare, [circa 1770]. BAnQ. P600,S5,PGC23.

Chapter Eight

8-0 *Aerial view of the Plains of Abraham*, 2016. ANBC.

8-1 *Plan de la ville et des fortifications de Québec*, 1808. LAC. 4128620.

8-2 *View up the St. Lawrence from the Citadel*, Québec. LAC. R9266-379. 2898290.

8-3 *Monument to Wolfe, Québec*, John Grant, 1832 or later. Watercolour on paper, 17.8 cm × 25.4 cm. Photographer: MNBAQ, Pierre-Luc Dufour. MNBAQ. Purchase. 1959.429.

8-4 *Translation des restes des Braves de 1760*, 1854. BAnQ. P600,S6,D1,P742.

8-5 *Des Braves Monument* 1909. ANBC.

8-6 *Overview of the Plains of Abraham in the early 20th century*. ANBC.

8-7 *His Excellence Lord Grey*. LAC. PA-042212. 3216349.

8-8 *Sector of the Des Braves Park before the landscaping work*, 1909. ANBC.

8-9 *Sir George Garneau*, [circa 1905]. BAnQ. P1000,S4,D83,PG18-2.

8-10 A *Some of Montcalm's soldiers at the pageants for Québec's Tricentenary, July 25, 1908*, artist unknown, for the Keystone View Company, 1909. Silver gelatin print, 8.9 × 17.8 cm (card); 8 × 15.3 cm (image). Photographer: MNBAQ, Patrick Altman. MNBAQ, donation from the Yves Beauregard Collection. 2006.2834.

8-10 B *Some of Montcalm's soldiers at the pageants for Québec's Tricentenary, July 25, 1908, artist unknown, for the Keystone View Company*, 1909. Silver gelatin print, 9 cm × 17.8 cm (card); 8 cm × 15.3 cm (image). Photographer: MNBAQ, Patrick Altman. MNBAQ, donation from the Yves Beauregard Collection. 2006.2833.

8-11 *Landscaping Plan for the Battlefields Park*, Frederick G. Todd, 1913. ANBC.

8-12 *Wolfe Monument*, 1909. ANBC.

8-13 *Plains of Abraham Trail*, 2016. ANBC.

Bibliography

B *Death certificate of Louis-Joseph Marquis de Montcalm* (detail). CE301, S1, P101, BAnQ.

Printed and bound in Canada
by Marquis Imprimeur
June 2022
Montmagny, Quebec.